P9-CQN-857

PARENTS GUIDE TO CHRISTIAN CONVERSATION ABOUT SEX

BY ERWIN J. KOLB

EDITOR / W. J. FIELDS

Concordia Publishing House

Saint Louis

BOOK FIVE of the Concordia Sex
Education Series

Other titles in the series:

BOOK ONE: I WONDER, I WONDER

BOOK TWO: WONDERFULLY MADE

BOOK THREE: TAKE THE HIGH ROAD

BOOK FOUR: LIFE CAN BE SEXUAL

BOOK SIX: CHRISTIAN VIEW OF SEX EDUCATION

Developed under the auspices of
The Family Life Committee
Board of Parish Education
The Lutheran Church — Missouri Synod

Concordia Publishing House, St. Louis, Missouri

© 1967 by Concordia Publishing House
Library of Congress Catalog Card No. 67-24876

MANUFACTURED IN THE UNITED STATES OF AMERICA

Editor's Foreword

This book is one of a series of six published by the Board of Parish Education of The Lutheran Church — Missouri Synod through its Family Life Committee. It is written specifically for parents, to be of assistance to them in the important task of guiding their children in the area of sex attitudes.

Four books in this series are directed to the children of various age levels: *I Wonder, I Wonder,* by Marguerite Kurth Frey, for kindergarten through grade 3; *Wonderfully Made,* by Ruth Stevenson Hummel, for grades 4 through 6; *Take the High Road,* by August J. Bueltmann, for junior high level; and *Life Can Be Sexual,* by Elmer N. Witt, for high schoolers.

The sixth volume of this series, *Christian View of Sex Education,* by Martin Wessler, is directed to pastors, teachers, youth workers, and parish planners to assist them in the structuring of a parish educational program in this area.

This series of books is concerned with much more than merely the biological facts of reproduction education. There are many such books, and good ones, on the market. This series of books is more concerned with the development of positive, Christian attitudes toward sex and with assisting boys and girls, men and women in fulfilling their roles as Christian boys and girls and Christian men and women.

Parents understand very well that this is primarily their responsibility. Often though, because of their own lack of insight, they feel inadequate to be effective in this area. This book is meant to assist parents in this important role.

This book keeps several things in mind. First of all, it understands that many parents have difficulty in communicating knowledge and attitudes and skills in the area of sex because they themselves do not feel free and relaxed. Their own knowledge many be limited to what they heard incidentally from others and from their own private experiences. From their own childhood they never had the opportunity to think of one's sex and sexuality being something very natural. The first three chapters of this book will help give parents a Christian understanding of sex for themselves and will apprise them of the role they must play in helping their children.

The book, furthermore, offers tangible help to parents who want to guide their children but don't know how to go about it. The last five chapters deal with specific age levels. Each chapter discusses some of the natural characteristics of the particular age level and then gives answers to some typical questions and concerns of that age level. The answers given are not meant to be used as such, but are meant to be guides to parents to show them how the question can be handled.

Sex education ideally belongs in the home. Children will learn about sex somewhere. For them not to do so is neither possible nor desirable. In the home, attitudes can be molded so that children not only know the facts of sex but also understand its meaning and place and Christian use.

Attitudes, we know well, are caught as much as they are taught. Family values are communicated indirectly as well as directly. This series of books keeps that in mind too. One little example. Whenever discussing the physical intimacies of marriage, this series of books does, and parents always should, use the terms "husband" and "wife" (rather than "man" and "woman") when talking about intercourse. Thus without saying so specifically, the impression is given also by implication that sexual intimacies belong to marriage.

Parents will want to purchase other books in this series that are geared to the age level of their children. After reading this book parents will be able to discuss with their children also the contents of the book written for them. When both have read in the area it makes for a common starting place that is not emotionally charged.

The medical facts of this book were checked by Dr. Charles Birdsall of the Department of Obstetrics and Gynecology in the McFarland Clinic in Ames, Iowa.

The author of this book was for many years a contributor to a magazine entitled *The Christian Parent*. He has been a pastor in a parish and is Dean of the Chapel at Concordia Teachers College, Seward, Nebr.

Special mention should be made of the Editorial Committee that assisted in the planning of this series: E. H. Ruprecht of Immanuel School in Valparaiso, Ind.; Frederick Nohl, of the Board of Parish Education, St. Louis, Mo.; and Walter Juergensen, Concordia Teachers College, Seward, Nebr. They were of constant encouragement and help to the editor.

W. J. FIELDS

Contents

Editor's
Foreword   3

     I.
A Christian
Understanding of Sex   11

     II.
Who Should
Talk About Sex?   23

     III.
How to
Talk About Sex   37

     IV.
Answering the First Questions
(up to 5 years)   51

     V.
Answering the Questions
Of Childhood (ages 6—11)   59

VI.
Answering the Questions
Of the Junior High Age
(ages 12—14)   74

VII.
Answering the Questions
Of the Senior High
And Young Adult   91

VIII.
Glossary
Of Terms   107

Annotated
Book List   119

Appendix   125

PARENTS GUIDE
TO
CHRISTIAN CONVERSATION ABOUT SEX

I.
A Christian Understanding of Sex

The word "sex" means different things to different people. To one person "sex" means intercourse, pregnancy, and childbirth. To someone else the word "sex" brings to mind the image of a shapely woman and stirs sexual desires. To still another "sex" is a subject too nasty and shameful to discuss. As one writer says, to many people "sex" is "a puzzle, a problem, uncomfortably accepted and uneasily explained to others." [1]

When one removes the connotations of the evil or shameful, however, the word "sex" describes something good and beautiful. It refers to gender, male or female, and includes the characteristics and functions of maleness and femaleness. Because of the exaggerated emphasis in our society on the physical aspects of sex the Christian context of the word has largely been lost. A Christian concept of the word "sex" includes:

1. sex as part of God's creation;
2. sex as that which makes possible the union of man and woman in the marriage relationship;
3. sex as the means for the creation and development of new life.

In order for Christian parents to talk to their children about sex in a way which could be called "Christian conversation about sex," they must speak from a Christian understanding of sex. The purpose of this chapter is to present this Christian view of sex.

11

Sex Is God's Creation

"Male and female created He them" (Gen. 1:27) writes the author of Genesis. Jesus adds in the New Testament, "He which made them at the beginning made them male and female" (Matt. 19:4). This simple but basic fact needs to be understood in order to have a Christian understanding of sex. Sex is God's idea, not man's. The unique physical structure with the organic and functional characteristics making a person male or female are part of God's design for human beings. This arrangement of maleness and femaleness, being of divine origin, is therefore in essence "very good." (Gen. 1:31)

The human body with its intricate design reveals some of the greatness and wisdom of its Creator. It became the vehicle of an even greater revelation of God when He revealed Himself in His Son, Jesus Christ. This is the foundation of the Christian faith, that the Word became flesh, that the Son of God totally and entirely became a human being so He could be the sacrifice for the sins of the world. The English author Hugh Warner makes this emphasis: "For all who study sex, therefore, those parts of the body most immediately relevant to its subject matter — the endocrine glands, ovaries, spermatozoa, uterus, and related organs — are parts of the whole 'human nature' through which the Christian revelation came." [2]

The Christian then regards sex, including the sex organs and their functions, with reverence and respect. He understands that no part of the body is "bad"; only its wrong use is. When the Christian confuses this, he opens the door for experiences such as that of Nancy.

Nancy began to be careless in her schoolwork. She was losing some of her warmth and friendship as she played with other children. Her alert teacher found a private moment to delve into the situation. Finally, 9-year-old Nancy broke down and confided: "I'm a bad girl now. Nothing matters much. When we were playing back in the woods we took off our clothes and looked at each other."

Understanding the normal curiosity of children, the teacher didn't consider the incident very significant until she talked to the parents. Then she discovered a possible reason for Nancy's deep feeling that she was a "naughty, dirty girl." Her parents had always kept the door locked when they were in the bedroom or bathroom. Nancy had never seen a person in the nude, and believed it evil to look at a naked body.

Nancy was suffering unnecessary pangs of conscience. She probably would have had difficulty for many years if someone had not helped her at this time. She needed to understand that God made her body and that no part of it was "dirty" or "unclean." Her sex organs were part of her femaleness. They equipped her to share one day in the union of marriage, to bring new life into the world, and to serve as a mother.

The Christian church in the past also has sometimes left the impression that sex is evil, an attitude which parents and teachers unconsciously pass on to succeeding generations. Often this attitude results in other wrong attitudes, such as shame when discussing sex organs or repugnancy at the thought of intercourse. A parent for example blushes when a child asks the innocent question, "Where did I come from?" An 18-year-old girl in a premarital counseling session asks with timid hesitation, "Is . . . it . . . sinful?" She is referring to intercourse but cannot get herself to say the word. A college freshman in a discussion of sex attitudes asks the leader, "You're married and have had intercourse. Doesn't it make you feel ashamed or guilty?" When a chuckle goes through the group, she continues, "Well, it's something that you don't want God standing there watching, do you?"

God created sex good. The improper use of sex does not make it impure any more than drunkenness makes drinking evil or gluttony makes eating sinful. What God Himself called "good," what He made for the honor of His name and the welfare of man, we have no right to call evil. As the study *Sex and the Church* summarizes it, sex "is to be accepted by the creature as a sacred, honored thing. It is to be received with thanksgiving and respected as a gift (1 Tim. 4:3, 4) which in many respects is more mysterious and wondrous than other gifts because it includes the gift of life itself." [3]

Man and Woman Complete Each Other

"The opposite sex" is an unfortunate misnomer. When God made human beings as male and female, He did so not simply for the sake of variety, nor that they would be different or "opposite." He rather made the two a team — "male and female created He them" (Gen. 1:27). "I will make him a helper fit for him" (Gen. 2:18). Each was made a part of the completed whole. Alone neither fulfills the entire purpose of God's creative design. They complete each other as suitable helpers, as complementary parts of one intended unit. For this reason it is much more accurate to refer to the other sex as the "complementary sex" rather than the "opposite sex."

This is apparent from the "built-in longing and desire" that the sexes have for each other. This need "penetrates into all phases of living." [4] Men and women need each other socially, psychologically, and spiritually, as well as physically. Marriage merges these complementary needs, so that ideally each partner finds his needs fulfilled in the other. This is true also physically. In sexual relationship the husband and wife become "one flesh." [5] The Bible uses the meaningful word "know" to describe the unique way in which the man and the woman become "one flesh" with each other. Here they reveal themselves and share a knowledge of themselves to each other that can be communicated in no other way.

The accomplishment of this "one flesh" relationship takes place in marriage. It cannot be successfully achieved outside of marriage. Two people find their complete fulfillment in each other only as they enter the permanent relationship of husband and wife and accept the full responsibilities of spouses to each other.

It should be said, however, that whereas the full purpose of sex is realized in marriage, marriage is not necessary for a happy and useful life. Some people do not have or do not take the opportunity to marry. This does not doom them to incomplete and unhappy lives. The unmarried person learns to control the sex impulses and drives which are otherwise satisfied in marriage, and finds fulfillment of life in other ways. He may find companionship with family or friends. The longing for children may be satisfied by working with children as a teacher, a social worker, or even a baby-sitter. A sense of usefulness and purpose may be achieved by direct service to others or by indirect service through church and community agencies. The unmarried, St. Paul points out (1 Cor. 7:32-34), may have a greater opportunity for special service to God because they do not have the concerns and cares of family life.

One understands the "first" purpose or plan for male and female more fully by recalling the purposes of marriage. The Christian church usually delineates the following three: companionship, physical relationships, and the procreation of children.

The "companionship" purpose of marriage is fulfilled as two people share their lives in love and become true "helpers" to each other. Gen. 2 concludes the story of the first marriage with the significant words, "Therefore a man leaves his father and his mother, and cleaves to his wife, and they become one flesh." In the New Testament, our Lord (Matt. 19:4-5), as well as the apostle Paul (Eph. 5:31), endorses this one-flesh relationship by repeating these words from Genesis. This union into one flesh involves more than physical intimacies. It includes the intimate and wonderful blending together of two personalities into a growing unity. This union is so precious that the writers of the New Testament compare it to the union between Christ and the church. St. Paul says, "I betrothed you to Christ to present you as a pure bride to her one husband" (2 Cor. 11:12). St. John speaks of the "bride, the wife of the Lamb" (Rev. 21:9). This Biblical figure not only illustrates the beautiful relationship between Christ and His church but becomes the model after which Christian marriage is to be patterned. St. Paul puts it in these words, "Husbands, love your wives, even as Christ also loved the church and gave Himself for it. . . ." (Eph. 5:25)

In the giving of themselves to each other, husband and wife find the deep meaning of love and a satisfying fulfillment of their marriage. The sexual surrender is an expression of their giving, a medium of their love. It is the debt each spouse owes the other, the privilege each can give the other (1 Cor. 7:3-4). William Hulme says, "It is the mediator for the total expression of union between husband and wife, even to the deepest spiritual dimension of this union." [6]

The physical aspect of marriage, which climaxes in sexual relationship, is to be a satisfying and enjoyable experience. The evidence of Scripture suggests strongly that marital sex is meant to be enjoyable (Prov. 5:18; Eccl. 9:9). Of this Dr. Feucht says, "In both the Old and New Testaments the sexual relationship is presented as an experience to be anticipated with pleasure and to be prepared for with affection and love, without necessarily having procreation as the conscious purpose." [7]

All of the purposes of marriage blend into one as husband and wife give themselves to each other in the act of sexual union. They share their lives in companionship. They unite their bodies in love. They join God in the creation of new life. God the Creator enables them to do together what neither of them can do alone.

Understanding sex within a Christian framework helps to free one from the restraints that sometimes frustrate the enjoyment of sexual relations. If one thinks of the physical aspects of married life as wrong or undesirable, he cannot enjoy them in uninhibited freedom and love.

Hugh Warner brings this home forcibly with the following example out of his own experience. A man had come to him for help, feeling that his wife no longer loved him because she was "shut up," as he put it: bitter in resentment, cross, and sharp with the children. As Warner counseled with the woman he discovered that she had lost her father when she was three and her mother had done all she could to protect her from the outside world by keeping her as close to herself as possible. One day, when she was 5, she and her mother stopped to look at a baby in a buggy on the street. "Where did that baby begin before it got into the buggy?" she innocently asked her mother. Her mother flushed and pulled her violently away by the hand. "That's a question," she said, "nice little girls don't ask. When you get bigger, you'll learn about it." The girl couldn't understand at the time what she had done to make her mother so cross, but she didn't want her mother to be like that again, so she didn't ask any more questions. There was something about babies and where they came from that made adults unhappy, she concluded. They didn't like to talk about it, so she wasn't going to stir up any unpleasantness.

As she grew older she learned more and more odd bits of information about human reproduction from older girls, but always in an atmosphere of secrecy. This helped to make her sure that her mother was right about this business. The end result was that later in her marriage she was not able to accept fully and gladly the physical expressions of married love. Her unconscious attitudes prevented the total surrender of herself. What began at the age of 5 and developed through her entire childhood became the root of her resentments and frigidity. It resulted in an unhappy marriage and an unhappy home.[8]

The divine purpose for the physical expression of sex is for the enhancement of marriage, the expression of love and unity of the spouses to each other, and for the sharing in the creation of life. This is a high and holy purpose.

Sex Relates to a Christian View of Life

Anyone who believes in some kind of supreme being can speak of sex as the creation of God. But this does not make his view or his attitude Christian. A person may recognize God as the creator of sex and still not see the Christian implication of its purpose. The Christian views his body not only as created by God but also as redeemed by Christ. He understands that by Holy Baptism he is associated with the death and resurrection of Jesus Christ and with Christ has risen to a newness of life. The Christian sees himself alive to God in Jesus Christ. He sees his "spiritual worship" as "presenting his body a living sacrifice, holy and acceptable to God" (Rom. 12:1). He believes that his body was "bought with a price" so that it could "glorify God." (1 Cor. 6:15-20)

The Christian's standards of sex behavior are part of the new life he has in Jesus Christ. It is easy to divorce one's behavior patterns from one's religion, to speak about the life in Christ on the one hand, and to live in response to one's desires and peer standards on the other. A pastor was talking to a girl about to have a baby out of wedlock. After a good cry, she became honest and open about what had happened, so the pastor asked: "What happens to a Christian girl like yourself when she sits in a parked car? You had a fine Christian home training, went to a Christian school, and remained active in your church. Now you are sorry for what you say you know is wrong. What happens out there?"

The girl spoke slowly, for she was trying to figure this thing out for herself. "I don't know. You just get carried away. 'Everyone does it,' he tells you. If you don't let him, he says you don't love him. One thing leads to another, and you just get carried away. And you know, you never think about God."

This girl might have been helped, many would agree, if she had been properly prepared. She could have been prepared with an understanding of what happens when one pets in a parked car; with an attitude of respect for her body and the boy's body; with a knowledge of love and sex that was marriage-centered. But what she needed most of all was to draw upon the power of the Christ who lived within her so that she be "not conformed to this world," but rather that she let God remold her life from within.

As the Christian lives his life under the certainty of God's love, he not only belongs entirely to God, but belongs to God in his entirety. He belongs to God not only in soul but also in body, not only in mind but also in sexual characteristics. The Christian is a new person, not simply in a general way, but as a new man or a new woman. All his purposes and functions as a man or as

18

a woman are an integral part of his new life in Christ. His body with all its physical functions has been renewed and reoriented by the redemptive activity of Jesus Christ. It is a holy temple, the dwelling place of God Himself.

Thus the Christian's view of sex ultimately rests upon the Christian view of life. Just as the culture of the modern world with its values resting on material things, on the enjoyment of pleasure, and on the satisfaction of desire runs counter to the Christian understanding of life, so this culture tends also to run counter to the Christian understanding of sex. The Christian must continually reexamine his values to see whether they are being influenced and patterned after this environment about him or by the Christ within him.

As one takes a serious look at our country, this is what he sees: The mass media — radio, television, movies, the printed page — overemphasize sex in such a way that they develop warped ideas of love, sex, and marriage. Recent movies for instance deal with subjects never before brought to the screen: lesbian lovers, homosexuals, rapists, misogynists, nymphomaniacs.[9] *Life* magazine said in an extensive article on the subject: "These motion pictures reflect a preoccupation with sex — and particularly its aberrations — that is unprecedented in the U. S."[10] It points out that sex stories have always been available back to the days of the medieval authors Chaucer and Boccaccio, but that they were generally kept behind closed doors. The novel *Fanny Hill* had to be smuggled in from Europe originally. Today one can buy it on any newsstand. Henry Miller's *Tropic of Cancer* was banned for 27 years but finally published in our country in 1961. It immediately became a best seller.

Sex is so overemphasized in parts of our society that the figure of a curvacious female in a skimpy bathing suit is used to attract attention on ads and billboards even though the female has nothing to do with the item being sold. One needs the "right measurements" to win a beauty contest and even to get some jobs.

In defense of this freedom some say, "It's better to bring sex out in the open than to hide it. I'd rather have the nude pictures sold on the magazine racks than have my children pass them around in secret." That may be democratic and tolerant, but making this kind of material so easily available gives approval to a warped treatment of sex. Allowing such a diet for the minds of youth helps to shape attitudes which are as loose and shoddy as the materials they see and hear.

In itself, for instance, there is nothing wrong with a story about a prostitute in a book or on the screen. But when the story glorifies this kind of life and glamorizes marital unfaithfulness, then it is damaging to the attitudes and standards of impressionable youth. Stories which treat love and marriage in a misshapen way are taking their toll in the lives of our adolescents.

What is the toll? We don't need to look long to find it. We see it in the conduct of our youth, as they experience the maturing of their sex desires and drives. Look for instance at the figures for premarital intercourse. One conservative estimate by a well-known psychologist is: The first coitus comes between 16 and 18, although as early as junior high for some; 25—35 percent of women and 50—75 percent of men have premarital coitus.[11] The famous Kinsey reports are more specific. His study reveals that by the age of 20, 75 percent of the males had premarital coitus.[12] Of the women marrying for the first time between 16 and 20, 47 percent were no longer virgins.[13] Harvard psychiatrist Dr. Graham B. Blaine, Jr., states that more than 50 percent of college women have had premarital relations.[14]

The toll can also be seen in the tremendous rise in the syphilis rate among teen-agers, 230 percent since 1956,[15] in the growing number of nonvirgin clubs, in the increasing number of teen-agers who "have to" get married, in the general loosening of sexual morals. But the toll often goes beyond premarriage problems. It carries over into marriage, resulting in unhappy marriage, infidelity, and divorce.

What is the solution? It is easy to oversimplify, but basic to any answer is a Christian view of sex which flows out of a Christian view of life. Only the man who has become a new creation

20

in Christ Jesus can fully appreciate his original creation. The man who is spiritually alive can joyfully and thankfully live out his physical life. The man who lives his life "in Christ" sees his life in its totality as an opportunity to glorify the Creator of that life.

This is important for all Christian parents to understand. If they desire to develop wholesome attitudes in their children, they need to begin with their own understanding of sex, for it is their own attitudes and understanding that they will pass on to their children.

FOOTNOTES FOR CHAPTER I

1. Adie Suehsdorf, ed., *What to Tell Your Children About Sex,* Child Study Association of America (New York: Permabooks, 1959), p. 4.

2. Hugh C. Warner, *The Christian View of Sex* (St. Louis: Concordia Publishing House, 1963), p. 4.

3. Oscar E. Feucht, ed., *Sex and the Church* (St. Louis: Concordia Publishing House, 1961), p. 215.

4. Ibid., p. 214

5. Gen. 2:24; Ex. 21:10; Lev. 13; Deut. 24:5; Matt. 19:5-6; Mark 10:6-8; 1 Cor. 7:2-6; Eph. 5:31.

6. William E. Hulme, *The Pastoral Care of Families* (New York: Abingdon Press, 1962), p. 26.

7. Feucht, p. 216. See also Jerome and Julia Rainer, *Sexual Pleasure in Marriage* (New York: Julian Messner, Inc., 1959).

8. Hugh C. Warner, *Puzzled Parents* (St. Louis: Concordia Publishing House, 1963), pp. 4–5.

9. See the glossary in the back of this book for an explanation and the correct pronunciation of terms.

10. Peter Bunsel, "Shocking Candor on the Screen, A Dilemma for the Family," *Life* (Feb. 23, 1962), pp. 88–102.

11. Elizabeth B. Hurlock, *Adolescent Development* (New York: McGraw-Hill Book Co., Inc., 1955), p. 418.

12. Alfred C. Kinsey, Wardell B. Pomeroy, and Clyde E. Martin, *Sexual Behavior in the Human Male* (Philadelphia: W. B. Saunders Co., 1948), p. 557.

13. Alfred C. Kinsey, Wardell B. Pomeroy, Cylde E. Martin, and Paul B. Gebhard, *Sexual Behavior in the Human Female* (Philadelphia: W. D. Saunders Co., 1952), p. 337.

14. Jeanie Loitman Barron, "Too Much Sex on Campus," *Reader's Digest* (May 1962), p. 29.

15. Reported by the U. S. Communicable Disease Center on Aug. 4, 1965. "Syphilis Among Youth up 230%," *The State*, Columbia, S. C. (Aug. 6, 1965), p. 6-A. In comparison, the years from 1956 to 1960 showed only an increase of 130% instead of the 230% for the years 1956—65, as reported by Cecelia A. Derchin, "Teen-agers and Venereal Diseases," *Children*, IX (July—August 1962), pp. 144—148.

II.
Who Should
Talk About Sex?

"Education is the school's job," Bill said when a neighbor invited him to a series of classes on how to give children proper sex education. "That's why we pay taxes," he went on. "And besides, I'm not qualified and I don't have the time to teach my children about sex."

That evening at dinner, Bill's 6-year-old daughter Sally heard Mother say: "I took a present over for the new baby at the Martins'. They are so happy it's a boy. He has long black hair and . . ."

"Mother," Sally broke in, "what's so different about a boy? Would you be happier if I were a boy?"

Bill and his wife both sat up with a start. "We are happy to have you as a girl," Bill said. He wanted to say more, but he was at a loss for words. Mother tried to ease out of the embarrassing situation by talking about the different clothes boys and girls wear. Sally was a little stunned by the experience, and Bill knew it.

That incident was enough. There was no further need of convincing Bill. He was ready for the parents' class. He had a part in the sex education of Sally, and he was beginning to realize it for the first time.

Parents are not the only ones responsible for explaining to a child the basic differences between boys and girls, for developing an understanding of the functioning of the human body. No one person or organization can adequately supply the necessary information and develop the proper attitudes. Many people and organizations are involved. The list includes: mother and father, brother and sister, grandparents, relatives, playmates, teachers, pastors, scout leaders, leaders in other community organizations, and many others. By their conversation and actions, the parents in the home, however, play the leading role, for they are involved in the child's growth and development from the beginning, or as one booklet puts it, "they have the privilege of living with their child, loving him, and sharing the daily round of experiences, feelings, and exchange of ideas." [1]

Parents Are First to Meet the Situation

"How many in your party, please?"

"Four" Mr. Black answered.

As soon as he said it, he heard a giggle from his 10-year-old daughter behind him. He contained himself until the hostess was gone, but then he turned to his still-smiling daughter with a look that demanded an explanation.

"She doesn't know, does she," the daughter explained, "that there are really five of us?"

The growing of a new baby inside Mother was a beautiful secret, a mysterious private miracle which Mr. and Mrs. Black shared with their children. They understood that wholesome attitudes toward sex grow through shared experiences of normal family living.

Parents are directly and primarily responsible for the training of the child. They are God's instruments and tools for this task.

As soon as the child is born, he begins to develop and learn. His body grows at a fantastic rate. He learns to sit, to crawl, to walk, to run, to talk, and to ask an endless number of questions. As his body develops and his mind learns, the child also develops in personality. He becomes a unique person with a set of attitudes and feelings all his own.

These feelings and attitudes are formed through all his relationships with people from the moment of his birth. The people most closely associated with him are usually his parents. Through their love and care and concern for him, they shape his attitudes toward people. As the child's hunger is satisfied and his uncomfortable diaper changed, as he hears pleasant sounds and feels safe in loving arms, he develops a feeling of security. Psychologists call this a "positive set, expectancy, or outlook." [2] The child learns to think of life as good because people do good things to him.

How the parents treat the child, how they work and play, talk and laugh with him, demonstrates their love and acceptance of him as a person. This all contributes to the development of the feeling of personal worth and confidence so necessary if he is to become a warm and friendly person, capable of accepting himself and others.

Many of the attitudes toward sex are shaped during these early years, for they are part of his feelings about himself and those around him. We might speak of the development of these early feelings as an unconscious imitation of the feelings of the parents. Advice for parents from a booklet prepared by a doctor says, "Parents' feelings affect the way the child feels about his body and its adolescent changes, about his own sex and the opposite sex, about babies, about marriage and family life, and about ways of expressing love." [3]

The parents, then, in these first years do not teach sex attitudes with words, but they do communicate with the "silent language of the home" which the child absorbs with his feelings. When, for example, a mother resents the unpleasantness of handling soiled diapers, the child may come to think of the function of elimination as "dirty" and "bad" even though the mother never says a word about it. The child senses how the mother feels and begins to feel the same way. Even later, when the mother can communicate in words which the child understands, what the child learns is based not only on the words themselves but also on the emotion and feeling which surround them.

Suppose Betsy slips during the toilet training period and makes a puddle on the living room rug. Her mother may spank and disgustedly say, "You are a naughty girl." This is "training" Betsy to have negative reactions to urination. But mother may instead say, "Did we slip, Betsy? We had better wash this out so it doesn't stain the rug. Maybe next time you can learn to go to the bathroom when you have to urinate." This kind of answer helps Betsy understand that urination is a natural function of the body, one which we must learn to control. So sex education is taking place through the silent language of the parents' actions as well as through their vocal conversation.

But when do parents begin to talk about sex organs and their functions? When does sex conversation become specific? As soon as parents talk to the child about any other part of the body. A mother may point to the nose and say, "nose," or to the other organs, "eye," "mouth," "tongue," "finger." There should be similar treatment for the other organs, "penis," "buttock," "breast," "navel," "vagina." Even though the parent does not explain the parts of the body and their functions at this time, he should use the correct names for them. As the child becomes more aware of his body and how the parts work, he will ask questions. The answers to these questions are important first conversations about sex. It is impossible to avoid discussion about sex until a certain age and then to take care of the matter in "one easy lesson," for the questions come as part of the many questions a child asks to satisfy his curiosity and his desire to learn and to know.

When the child is old enough to play with neighborhood children and with schoolmates, he will talk about sex with them. He will compare what his parents have told him with what the other children know. He will ask more questions and share what he knows. In this childhood conversation about sex, he may absorb incorrect knowledge, or uncertain and confusing ideas. Parents need to keep the child's confidence and continue the conversations about sex through the years so that he will share the impressions and knowledge he receives from his friends. This enables the parents to correct wrong ideas and shape positive attitudes. If parents avoid the child's questions or answer with old clichés and evasions, they will cut themselves off from the child and cannot expect him to come to them for help when he needs forthright answers. When a child is puzzled about his mother's "monthly sickness," and confused about how the stork brought him, he could easily develop attitudes which conceive of sex as some shadowy mystery about which it is improper or even evil to speak openly.

An illustration of this is the story of Jenny which appears in *Parents' Privilege*,[4] one of the excellent booklets published by the American Medical Association on sex education. Whenever Jenny brought home a school paper with a star, her mother hugged and patted her and called her "honey." She did the same when her friends praised Jenny for her fine manners and dancing skill. One day Mrs. Brown discovered Jenny undressed while playing doctor with a girl friend. "I'm so ashamed of you," she said. "How can I love a little girl who is so naughty?" After this Jenny was never quite sure how any new game or escapade would be received by her mother, and she grew very anxious about her play and her schoolwork. How could Jenny ask her mother about anything connected with her body or its functions?

Information about sex that is not surrounded by understanding love may lead to gruesome and terrifying concepts for the child. When parents talk about the body and its functions in a natural and wholesome way, they are helping the child develop this same attitude. If they display a consistent spirit of reverence toward sex and the other sex, the child will develop such an attitude too. No one can ever adequately replace parents in this intimate and delicate learning situation.

A child's attitude toward sex includes his feelings about his own body and his role as male or female, his feelings about the other sex, and the relationships that are involved in love and marriage. Christian parents are concerned that these attitudes be consistent with a Christian understanding of sex that honors God as the Creator, Redeemer, and Sanctifier of our bodies.

The child's attitudes can, however, be Christian only when the child himself is a Christian. This should always be the parents' primary concern. Parents want their child to grow up healthy not merely physically, emotionally, and mentally, but also spiritually. For this they must bring the child into a living and vital relationship with Jesus Christ. Through Baptism he becomes linked up with the very life of God, living under His constant love and forgiveness. His response is the response of love and dedication to Jesus Christ. He must see this operating now in his parents, who demonstrate for him how to put this love into action and who themselves display attitudes which are consistent with Christian concepts and beliefs.

Parents Must Cope with Their Own Problems

Some parents are reluctant to talk to their children about sex because they feel inadequate to do so. They may not be sure of their knowledge of the facts, or they may feel uncomfortable talking about the sex organs and their functions. Some parents have emotional blocks as a result of unfortunate early experiences with sex. Such parents often impose their own misconceptions and inhibitions on the child, either by actually communicating their attitudes, or by avoiding the topic entirely. Parents who feel this problem may do at least these three things:

1. They may read good books about sex until they are sure of the correct information. The last chapters of this book suggest some approaches to putting accurate information into intimate conversation with children. Other books in this series are more specific as they aim at a defined age level:

For kindergarten and grades 1-2-3: *I Wonder, I Wonder*
For grades 4-5-6: *Wonderfully Made: What Pre-Teens Want to Know*
For grades 7-8-9: *Take the High Road*
For grades 10-11-12: *Life Can Be Sexual*

2. They may talk about this with their spouse or close friends. Using the vocabulary of sex in conversation with other

adults is good preparation for talking to a child. It is difficult to use words in normal conversation that are unfamiliar and associated with shame or guilt. Understanding this, one mother practiced by talking to herself and the baby at bath time, something like this: "Now we'll wash the little hands and fingers and then we get the feet and the tiny toes. And we mustn't forget the little penis and the rosy buttocks." Hearing herself say the words prepared her for using them later when she had to explain them.

3. They may join a study or discussion group of other parents who are interested in sex education and child development. This could well be a couples club, a parent-teacher group, a YMCA or YWCA, or any other church or community organization. Participating in such a group gives parents the opportunity to lose some of their shyness in discussing sex topics, to practice their vocabulary, and to learn approaches from other parents.

Another problem which parents have in developing sex attitudes is the limitation imposed by their relationship to each other. If there is friction and quarreling between them, the parents cannot teach the meaning of love and consideration. The marriage relationship sets the tone of the home. If there is respect and understanding, patience and love between husband and wife, the stage is set for the child to learn the same virtues. The child's attitudes toward sex are influenced by the atmosphere of the home; the two are inseparably linked together. The one influences the other. The child's concepts of the man and his place in life, of the woman and her function, are determined largely by his own parents.

If there is lack of harmony and unity in their marriage, the parents should seek assistance to achieve it both for the sake of their own marriage and for the sake of the children. Good books help, but they often are not enough by themselves. Personal counseling with a pastor, a counselor, or a psychiatrist is sometimes necessary. Talking to other married couples honestly and frankly may aid them to see the real problem. The concerned couple that understands that the child seldom rises above the potential set by the example of its parents will use whatever means are available to help them build a strong home life.

One of the serious problems in sex education is the broken home, where there is only one parent — often the mother — to train the child. It is serious because a child needs both a father and a mother for the normal development of his attitudes. Psychologists tell us that it works something like this. A child of 4 or 5, while he may love both parents, wants to marry the one of the opposite sex and becomes a rival of the same-sexed parent. In a year or so he gives up this impossible dream and takes the parent of his own sex as his model. "This is a big step toward satisfied identification with his own sex and pleasurable acceptance of being a boy, or being a girl." [5] As the child associates with other boys and girls, other steps follow to help achieve this "sexual identification," which is considered the major developmental task of the preadolescent period. When one of the parents is missing from the home, the child is deprived of the opportunity of relating to that parent, and the normal development is frustrated. The child has difficulty in properly understanding and accepting the role of the male and female and in relating to each of them. When one of the parents is missing, the remaining parent would do well to find a "substitute parent." For instance, if there is no father, the mother should find some male to fill the father role for the child, a male relative perhaps, or a friend or neighbor. It should be someone whom the child can respect and admire and spend some time with.

Many communities have chapters of Parents Without Partners, an organization with headquarters at 80 Fifth Ave., New York 10011. This organization is set up to offer such help. Some churches, especially in metropolitan areas, have developed their own organizations along this line.

In concluding this brief section on the problems parents face in leading their children to wholesome sex attitudes, it might be said, lest some parents become discouraged, that although all parents make mistakes, children are flexible enough to overcome most of them. Children will go elsewhere to get the information the home did not supply; they will seek to fill their unmet need of understanding and love in substitute ways. They are also capable of living with some of the same inadequate attitudes which handicapped the parents. But this realization should not settle the parents into a complacent attitude, nor justify their failures. When parents realize their shortcomings and mistakes, they should make what amends are still possible within their limitations and within the time that remains to do it. The place to begin is in giving the child as much acceptance, love, and understanding as possible. A home where father and mother love each other deeply and are loyal and considerate provides the setting for the kind of relationship where there can be some Christian conversation about sex.

The School Builds on the Parents' Foundation

Parents don't always realize that, when a child starts school, the opinion of the teacher usually carries more weight than that of the parent. At this age the school and the individual teacher play an important role in the development of proper attitudes toward sex. The school's contribution is somewhat different from that of the home, of course. The school builds on the foundation already established in the home and provides information in a more impersonal setting. With objective presentations and discussions the school can help to correct misconceptions the child may have and answer questions that he was reluctant to ask his parent. Unless he has been able to talk freely and frankly with his parents through the years, the teen-ager, especially, finds it difficult to discuss sex with his parents. The school is the authority against which he can check the information and attitudes which his peers supply. It also provides for the total group a common bond of knowledge on the subject so that there is less room for the sharing of misconceptions.

Much of the contribution of the school in this area has been called the "integrated approach," [6] wherein sex education is built into the everyday teaching of children as they go through the grades. Much sex education also occurs in the informal relationships between teacher and pupil outside the classroom. A boy, for example, will often get more help from his coach than from any other adult with whom he has contact. Because much of sex education takes place in these personal interrelationships of pupil and teacher, the qualifications of the teacher are very important. A committee of the New York State Department of Education reported "that the personalities of the parents and teachers, and their own behavior, did more to influence attitudes and practices of young people than any other factor" (ibid.). The personality traits that it considered important were: emotional maturity, personal character which boys and girls can respect, and sympathetic understanding of boys and girls.

Schools ought to go beyond the "integrated approach" and informal teaching, however. They should have programs of formal instruction for the various age levels to inform the child about the human body, reproduction, the roles of male and female, love and marriage. A school may set up a program in which the elementary grades include units of sex instruction in health education or science classes. Junior high courses may include units on personality growth and boy-girl relations. The high school may offer classes on courtship, marriage, and parenthood. The establishment of such a program must be preceded and accompanied by the proper preparation in the community in order to ready the homes and the community for what is happening. Care must be taken to avoid antagonism, for teaching these subjects is still objected to by many.

In one small town some high school parents, on the basis of reports from their children, formally protested the teaching of a Family Living course. The basis of the protest was that it was being taught by an unmarried woman. When the class studied pictures of the human anatomy, the senior boys jokingly made lewd comments. The principal investigated and changed the one unit of the course. The boys were separated and taught by a man whom they respected.

The fear which causes parents at times to object to sex education in formal classes is the fear that knowledge and discussion about sex will cause an unwholesome preoccupation with sex that will lead to "bad" habits. But the opposite may be true. It is the child whose normal curiosity has not been satisfied who may express his uneasy ignorance in dirty sex talk and toilet scribblings. In one school where there was an unwholesome epidemic of sex talk in the fifth grade, parents and teachers agreed to show the film *Human Growth*. After it had been shown and the children's questions freely answered, the improper remarks and the whispering in corners stopped. One little boy, who had been a ringleader, even thanked the teacher for showing the film and helping him find out what he wanted to know.[7]

Parents should know what their school is doing in sex education and cooperate with it in every way they can, by working with the teachers instead of against them. Christian parents are concerned that a good program of sex education is established in their school, not only because they want the best for their own child, but also because they want this for all the children of their congregation or community, especially for those whose parents fail to do the job. They know that good training in this area is a benefit to all.

Community Organizations Assist

In addition to parents and teachers, the organizations of the community also have a part in the total development of the child's sex attitudes. Although this is not a handbook on community organizations, this book does want to point out to parents that community organizations do contribute to the sex training of the child.

Many girls, for instance, learn the facts about menstruation for the first time when they see a movie shown by their Girl Scout troop or the parent-teacher organization of their school. A nurse is usually on hand to answer questions after the movie, and often the girls are given one of the many free booklets available from the producers of sanitary napkins.[8]

In some areas parent-teacher organizations give excellent help to parents through lectures, discussions, and courses on sex education and related subjects. Often community agencies such as mental health centers or hospitals offer special courses for expectant parents. These are but a few of the ways in which community agencies help not only the child but the parent who guides the child. The wise parent will make use of such help.

The chief contribution of these community organizations to the sex guidance of the child lies in filling in the gaps in what the home and the school have already done, and in continuing to encourage growth in understanding. Much of this is done through the personal contact between the leaders and workers in these organizations and the child as they work together in wholesome relationship. Parents should be aware of this contribution and appreciate it.

The Church Shares in the Responsibility

"What does 'weaned' mean?" "Was 'Virgin' Mary's first name?" Such questions addressed to a church-school teacher need answers. And the answers are a form of sex education provided by the church.

The church has a very special responsibility in this area. It begins with a positive view of sex as God-given and therefore in itself good. Building on this truth, it provides help for people of all ages to respect their bodies and develop wholesome attitudes toward their own sex and the other sex. It assists young people in shaping their behavior patterns commensurate with the ultimate goal of love, courtship, and romance and to prepare themselves for marriage with Christian attitudes toward it. It guides couples into a Christian approach to marriage and assists parents in leading their children to a wholesome Christian view of sex.

There are many opportunities and means by which the church makes its contribution to sex education. In its preaching and teaching it must continually reflect a Christian concept of sex. The pastor in his classes for church membership has opportunities to discuss specifically such things as dating, courtship, petting, premarital sex relations, and marriage from a Christian point of view.

One pastor tells of leading a discussion with his young people on Christian conduct on a date. The questions of the young people led to a discussion of the entire area of courtship relationships. Afterward one boy said, "I have always thought everybody nowadays had premarital sex relations. Now I know that some of us can be different because we believe in Christ." This is one of the practical results of the church's concern for developing a Christian view of sex, young people strengthening each other to meet the temptations of sex and mutually supporting each other in the living of their Christian lives. All Christians need this witness to each other in order to reinforce their faith and to edify each other in their mutual development.

Much excellent sex education material is published in magazines, pamphlets, and books. Much of it, however, lacks Christian content and motivation. The difficulty for the Christian is that as he reads this literature he may think of sex education apart from the Christian framework, thus dividing the secular and the sacred. The church's responsibility is to help parents see that there is no such distinction. The secular too (that includes sex), has been redeemed and is therefore sacred.

Pastors, teachers, and church workers will find further discussion and help in the book in this series designed for leaders: *Christian View of Sex Education*, by Martin Wessler.

FOOTNOTES FOR CHAPTER II

1. Marion O. Lerrigo and Michael A. Cassidy, *Your Child from 9 to 12* (Chicago: Budlong Press Co., 1964), Foreword, n. p.
2. Armin Grams, *Children and Their Parents* (Minneapolis, Minn.: T. S. Denison & Co., 1963), p. 66.
3. Lerrigo and Cassidy, p. 23.
4. Marion O. Lerrigo and Helen Southard, *Parents' Responsibility* (Chicago: American Medical Association, 1962), p. 12.

5. Lerrigo and Cassidy, p. 9.

6. Helen I. Driver, ed., *Sex Guidance for Your Child: A Parent Handbook* (Madison, Wis.: Monona Publication, 1960), pp. 93–107.

7. Lerrigo and Cassidy, p. 20.

8. a. *Complete Educational Portfolio on Menstrual Hygiene.* Contains teachers guide, film brochure, and booklets titled *Growing Up and Liking It* and *How Shall I Tell My Daughter?* Free to teachers from Personal Products Co., Milltown, N. J. 08850.

   b. *The Tampax Educational Kit.* Contains teachers guides, booklets titled *Accent on You* and *It's Time You Knew.* Free to teachers from Tampax, Inc., 161 E. 42nd St., New York, N. Y. 10017.

   c. *Very Personally Yours.* A kit to help teachers and parents prepare girls for the beginning of menstruation. Contains pamphlets and a sampling of Kotex products. Available at 50 cents from Educational Department, Kimberly-Clark Corp., Neenah, Wis. 54956.

III.
How to
Talk About Sex

Sex education is more than conversation about sex. Sex education involves a series of experiences through which the child comes to understand the facts of human life and develops wholesome attitudes toward himself and others. While there are some formal teaching situations, most of these experiences are routine happenings and normal conversations which make up much of daily family living. The growing child's curiosity and inquiring mind spawns a continuous line of questions: "Why did Jacob have four wives?" "Will hair grow under my arms?" "Why is Pam different than I am?" "What is this?" as he places his fingers on his breast or navel. Hundreds of questions like these, and the actions and conversations which follow form the core of knowledge and feelings that add up to sex education.

How do parents answer these questions? It is not possible to give a "canned" answer to every question, even though it might seem as though chapters 4 through 7 of this book will be trying to do this. These chapters offer sample demonstrations of possible ways to answer specific questions. More important, however, are the general principles which apply to all situations which are discussed in this chapter under the headings: Be ready, Be natural, Be reverent, Be honest, Be modest. The pattern of this chapter is an expanded outline. The basic material are 15 pointed suggestions, each of which is expanded with brief comment or illustration. Some of the thoughts have already been discussed but are included in the outline for completeness.

Be Ready

As soon as a child is born, sex education begins, as does all child training. The method of training is the language of love, concern, and acceptance. Before he can utter a word, the child has learned to feel. He has already had his first experiences with love or rejection by others, with their respect for him and his needs, with their concern for his body. It is these experiences shaped by the attitudes and actions of the parents that become the foundation upon which sex attitudes are built.

When it is time to start bladder and bowel control, the parents' own attitude toward the "full pants" or the "puddle of mistake" affects the child. If the parents are especially harsh and use words like "nasty" and "naughty," the child may connect these concepts to his organs of elimination and comes to think of his genitals as "nasty." Christian parents need to learn patience, as difficult as it is at times, and try not to force control.

EXPECT AND INITIATE QUESTIONS

There is no way of knowing when they will come, but certain basic questions about sex will be asked. These questions grow out of the natural curiosity of a child about the differences between boys and girls, where babies come from, and the father's part in the process. The child must have answers for these questions. It is better if he gets them correctly from his own parents rather than from other children or from trashy literature. As long as parents give honest, forthright answers and keep the relationship with their child one of warm trust and confidence, the questions will keep coming.

As a 10-year-old girl was getting ready to leave home for 2 weeks at camp, she came to sit on her father's lap for a little talk while they were still together. As she rubbed her hand over his arm, she commented, "Why do men have so much hair on their arms?"

"Because this is a mark of being a man," he said. However, instead of stopping he went on, for he saw an opening by which he could initiate the discussion that he wanted. "Women have other marks which God has made to show that they are women."

"Like what?" she asked. This was his opportunity. He went on to explain the development of her breasts and told her why she would soon begin to menstruate.

Some people think that it is better for mothers to talk to their daughters about this and for fathers to talk to boys. While this may be true for some, ideally either parent can talk to either child. Determining factors are the ability to speak openly on the subject, the personal relationship that exists, and the opportunities that arise.

Parents must anticipate questions and at times initiate them. When questions do not come voluntarily, a little probing may be in order to overcome some of the hesitancy for open discussion. If a small girl, for example, walks around holding a stick in front of her, or a boy peeks into the bedroom when others are dressing or makes excuses to get things from the bathroom when someone is using it, these may be signals that the child needs to discuss the differences in male or female but is afraid to bring up the subject.

Dr. Lerrigo suggests that one way of taking the initiative is to make a remark like, "You know, when I was a bit younger than you are, I thought a baby started when a boy kissed a girl. What did you think when you were younger?" [1] The child then has the opportunity to talk about the ideas he has had without admitting his present ignorance. Letting the child first give his own ideas helps to know what it is that he needs to know now. Another opportunity presents itself when a child repeats a sexy joke that he has heard. Instead of scolding, a parent may ask what it means and lead into a discussion. Other springboards for discussion come through some neighborhood happening or news event which has aroused the child's interest: a new baby is born, a neighbor is pregnant, a pet dog has puppies.

LISTEN WHEN THEY ASK

Listening is as important as explaining. When a small child asks a question, he is curious about a single, specific thing. While the parents may be able and eager to give a detailed explanation, with all the ramifications, the youngster wants only a few facts given in a direct and honest way. The small child's listening interest normally lasts for about 30 seconds. What he isn't told in 30 seconds he usually is not interested in knowing at that time. As he gets older, he will listen longer and ask more questions, but he will listen only until his curiosity at that moment is satisfied.

The adolescent often asks with more than his words. He may seek information by his actions and interest, and his questions may be only peripheral. He asks questions around the point to test his parents, to determine whether it is safe to go further. Parents who really listen will catch the signals and encourage the conversation, even prodding with other questions if he doesn't muster up the courage to go all the way.

One needs to be careful, however, not to read his own adult understanding into a question. "Can I see where the baby comes out?" is normally an innocent question, free of any lewd thoughts. A child accepts the human body and its system of reproduction as natural unless he has been taught to think that there is something "different" or secretive about it.

As a mother or father listens carefully to the words and tries to feel the needs of the child, he or she alone will know best how to answer the questions. There is some danger in trying to tell too much too early. This could stimulate interest beyond the child's readiness or make sex gruesome and frightful to him. One mother was showing her 6-year-old the pictures in a book about the sperm and egg meeting and beginning to grow. She ex-

40

plained it all and showed him a cutaway picture of the baby growing in the uterus. The boy had enough and said, "Let's not read any more, Mother. That's not pretty." The child was evidently not ready. The best guide is the questions and the interest of the child.

Be Natural

AVOID SHOWING SHAME OR SHOCK

Parents communicate sex guidance not only through words but also through their reactions and feelings. If they find it difficult to discuss a question, or blush and grope for words, the child catches a signal that there is something shameful about sex. When his mother found Jim looking at pictures of a nude woman in a medical book, she told him she was terribly shocked that he would do such a thing. Jim caught the feeling which came with the words — the naked body is bad. These attitudes toward sex make it more difficult for a child, as he grows up, to accept his manliness or womanliness as a natural, wholesome part of his being.

AVOID HARSH TREATMENT

Dorothy Baruch gives two illustrations of what harsh treatment, as a reaction to sex experimentation, can do to the emotional lives of children.[2]

As a child, James was caught playing with his penis. His father said, "If I catch you playing with yourself again, I'll break every bone in your body. You'll ruin yourself." Well, James thought he had ruined himself, and as he grew into the teens he had a hidden fear about it. Unconsciously he was driven to try to prove that his father was wrong and that he had not ruined himself. So he rushed from one sex exploit to another.

The other example is the story of Lorna. While sitting on the grass in the yard at the age of 3, she was caught examining her genitals. Her mother said rather sharply, "Keep your fingers away from there, Lorna." Later she picked her up, cuddled her and repeated expressions like, "Keeping clean," "not ever touch," and "not to make yourself sore." Similar episodes followed through the years. When Lorna grew up and married, she could enjoy the arms of her husband around her, but when he approached sexual intercourse, Lorna said, "Something makes me turn away." The attitude that her mother had instilled about her genitals had taken its toll and Lorna was paying for it with an unhappy marriage relationship.

Children are very resilient and often able to overcome the fears of parents, but James and Lorna are examples of what may happen. When a child is "caught" in what adults have labeled as "bad" or "terrible," the parents need to be cautious about overly harsh treatment. In discussing it, it is best to be as natural as possible, remembering the danger of developing attitudes which cause feelings of excessive fear and shame.

ACCEPT SEX AND ORGANS OF ELIMINATION AS GOOD

Many parents find it difficult to keep from showing shock and want to use harsh treatment because they grew up connecting evil with the genitals. Such a person has not learned that even urination and bowel movements are unique and intricate operations of the human body. There is nothing evil about the sex organs themselves. God had made every organ good and dependent upon each other. St. Paul speaks of them this way: "God arranged the organs in the body, each one of them, as He chose . . . and our unpresentable parts are treated with greater modesty, which our more presentable parts do not require." (1 Cor. 12: 18-24)

The genitals are treated with modesty but this does not make them bad. They can be misused for lust and sensuality, but this does not make them evil. When they are used by the Christian according to God's plan and purpose they are good and bring honor to their Creator.

Be Reverent

We have spoken of this previously, but we emphasize it again. God in a wisdom which surpasses all science created the human body. He designed it. He planned its total functioning. The Christian cares for his body as a sacred trust from the Almighty. Whenever he answers questions about sex, he does so with a sense of respect and reverence for the wonderful gift the body is. When parents believe and live this attitude, their children will catch it too.

SPEAK OF PARENTHOOD AS THE PRIVILEGE OF SHARING IN A MIRACLE

Children develop their ideas about parenthood through living with their own parents. When they live in a home where children are considered a privileged trust from God, they will learn the significance of responsible parenthood. When their own home life is happy, they will be ready to accept parenthood as a happy life of service to God. If, however, they hear constant complaining about the difficulties of parenthood and the high cost of families, they may grow up with negative reactions to having families of their own.

Parents can contribute much to a child's Christian view of sex by pointing out to him that having a baby is sharing with God in the miracle of creation. When they explain how the baby is formed through the male sperm and female ovum, and is nourished through the intricate system of placenta and umbilical cord, they should do it with a sense of wonder. Parents who do this when speaking of other organs or functions of the body may neglect to do it when it comes to sex organs and sex functions. It is easy for some to speak with amazement about the intricate structure and operation of the eye or ear but they hesitate to speak in the same way about other organs such as the female breast. An article in *Reader's Digest* speaks of the breast as one of the "wonders of science." [3] For 2 to 4 days after the birth of a baby the breast produces a yellowish substance so that the nursing baby may clear the mucus from its digestive system and help protect it from disease. Then special cells make milk out of the only raw material available, blood. This is a stupendous chemical achievement, which science cannot duplicate. The chemical components of blood are totally unlike those of milk, and how the change takes place is a mystery. The female breast is more than a sex symbol; it is an amazing, functional creation which speaks of the wisdom and majesty of God.

SPEAK OF SEX IN THE FRAMEWORK OF LOVE AND MARRIAGE

Parents who are Christian have a special responsibility and a sacred privilege in the education of their children by virtue of their relationship to Christ. The Christian's central purpose in child training is to lead the child to believe in Jesus Christ as Savior. The result of this faith is obedience — the obedience of service to Christ as the Lord of life and living.

St. Paul speaks very specifically about this to his congregation at Corinth: You are bought with a price. Your body is the temple of God. Keep your body holy and do not pollute it with sexual sins. (1 Cor. 6)

When a Christian family discusses sex, they speak as people who have been "sanctified in Christ Jesus" (1 Cor. 1:2). They are able to discuss the sex organs and their functions from a shared belief that their bodies are the temples of God, which they use to honor Him.

Christian parents help their children achieve a wholesome respect for their own bodies and the bodies of others, learning to control their sex desires and to reserve the use of the mating ability for the surrender of marriage.

Be Honest

GIVE SIMPLE, DIRECT ANSWERS

A 6-year-old boy told his teacher that he and Mary had decided to get married. The teacher played the game and asked how he would support her. The boy figured that if they put their allowances together they could get by.

The teacher went one step further. "But what will you do if a baby comes?" "Oh, we figured that out, too," he confidently answered. "When we see the doctor come with his little black bag, we'll hide under the bed."

Imagine what this boy was told about babies and where they come from! He will have to unlearn the mistaken concepts before he can learn the truth. But why must a child go through this learning the wrong way, unlearning it, and then learning the truth? It is much easier to tell the truth from the beginning, with simple, direct answers to the first questions. As the child grows older, more insights may be added to what he already knows.

There is no place for the stork story, the doctor's black bag, or any of the other stories that are sometimes told to children to avoid telling them the truth. Some people still believe that sex information causes a child to become overly interested in sex and will lead him to all sorts of sexual experimentation. But when a child is given simple, straightforward answers to satisfy the curiosity of his age, he is helped to accept sex without any warped interest and can seek more information as he gets older and more curious.

"The birds and the bees" approach, although it can be used to advantage, is also an evasion of a direct and honest telling of the facts. Many a child has seen kittens or puppies nursing and has asked questions as to whether they were "eating their mother." This is a splendid opportunity to speak about how God provides milk for babies in the breasts of their mothers until they are old enough to drink instead of suck. Another of the more obvious opportunities from nature is when a pet or farm animal gives birth to offspring. Care must be taken, however, not to equate animals with humans. Biologically they mate in a similar way, but people mate out of love and desire for each other, and not simply out of instinct.

The quickest way to lose a child's confidence and make it difficult for him to ask further questions is to evade questions or to lie in the answers. When it is later discovered that the answer was a deliberate deception, confidence is destroyed and it is not easily restored. When parents evade questions by saying, "You're too young to know," or "you shouldn't ask such questions at your age," the child concludes that there are no answers here for his questions. To keep an open door of trust and encouragement, parents must be consistent in giving fair and honest answers. If they do not know the right answers, it is easy to say this frankly and together with the child to seek the correct answer. To say "later" is the same as not giving an answer at all. The child who asks does not want to know "later"; he wants to know when he asks.

But it takes more than just honest answers to keep confidence. The child must respect his parents and be sure of their love. He must feel that even though he doesn't fully understand why his parents set a certain restriction or forbid a particular request he knows that they love him. A child will respect and love his parents when he knows and feels that they respect him and trust him. This is the kind of relationship which allows free conversation about intimate and personal matters.

If this relationship is not developed at a young age, it cannot be developed very easily in the teen-ager, and the parents will lose many opportunities to answer questions and help their child with his problems.

Mrs. Selma Fraiberg, a child psychotherapist who teaches at Tulane University, tells of a 6-year-old who placed a cucumber seed by a telephone pole. When asked why he did it he replied, "So's me and Polly can have a baby next summer." [4] This boy did not know how babies were made, or at least he was pretty confused. And it was probably due, in part at least, to his parents' failure to give simple, direct, honest answers to his specific questions.

It is easier to be honest when frank and specific words rather than deceptive ones are used. When the parts of the body are explained to a 2- or 3-year-old, or the functions of the body to a 4- or 5-year-old, it is essential to use the correct words. Just as one uses the correct words when referring to other parts of the body, like a toe or an ankle or elbow, so one can just as easily and simply say the correct word when referring to the genitals or the anus. If parents are willing to learn and use these words, they make it easier for their child to know how to ask questions. It is difficult to discuss his problems and worries about sex when he does not know the proper words to use.

If a child does not learn these correct words at home, he will learn other words from playmates in school, on the playground, or in the back alley. If he knows only "tinkle" or "wee-wee" he will find it difficult to use the word "urinate" with his parents because he never hears them say it. The same applies to all the organs of the body and their functions. For all the sex organs and their functions there are four-letter words which are considered vulgar but which people still learn as they grow up. How can the child ask questions using this vocabulary when it is considered filthy? He doesn't even want his parents to know that he can use such words.

This is not to say that it is poor training to use words like "grunt" or "tinkle" with a 3-year-old, or to say "go to the toilet" instead of urinate, but rather that parents must teach the proper terms by using them in the home as the child grows up and needs them. At various age levels he must hear, come to understand, and be able to use words like penis, urinate, navel, bowel movement, vulva, vagina, uterus, womb, menstruate, testicle, scrotum, pregnant, and later: adultery, intercourse, homosexual, masturbation, and so on. This language forms the basis for discussion. Without it there can be little Christian conversation about sex. One boy summed it up when he said, "I wouldn't trust myself to ask other adults about sex. If I used the wrong word, they'd drop dead from shock!"[5]

But what if parents try to use the right words and the child still brings home the vulgar words? They should be thankful that he feels free and confident to tell them about these words. This gives them an opportunity to discuss the words and to point out that it is better to use the proper ones. One family did this by letting the family discuss the matter together and agree which were the best words for them to use. Thus they made this a family learning experience in which positive attitudes were being molded.

Be Modest

ACCEPT THE NUDE BODY WITHOUT SHAME

What fun for a 2-year-old! Bath is finished. The body is fresh and clean. Now to wiggle away from mother for a minute and run through the house, barefoot and bare-bottom. What if there are ladies in the other room who see a naked boy run past them? The boy doesn't mind, and the sensible ladies who happen to be there don't either. Self-consciousness is not a characteristic of a 2-year-old and to reprimand him as if he had done something wrong will at best confuse him, and at worst cause him to think that exposure of one's nakedness is in itself indecent.

One of the first questions that a child asks about the other sex is the differences in physical makeup. This curiosity may be satisfied by allowing him to see the nude body of the opposite sex, in such ways as bathing small children together, letting one watch diaper changes, dressing together, and so forth. Some parents allow their child to see them in the nude. He will think nothing of this when he is very small, but when he gets to be 3 years and older the naked body may be gruesome or fearful to him. It is usually better to use other ways than one's own body. If a child walks into the bedroom, however, when a parent is partially naked, he need not be alarmed. Rather, he may treat

48

the matter casually and say something like, "Did you forget to knock?" or "Did I forget to close the door?"

Modesty will normally develop as a child learns to accept the way of life set by the culture in which we live, and comes to respect the privacy of the parts of the body that are normally clothed, especially the parts of the body created for procreation and the feeding of the newly born. Some primitive peoples never cover the breasts but only the genitals. This is the accepted pattern in their culture. For them modesty doesn't have all the connotations it has for us Americans.

The home and the example of the parents set a standard of modesty which a child gradually comes to make his own by unconscious imitation. How much he finally accepts and practices is dependent upon many factors, some known — as the relationship and respect in the home — and some quite unknown.

In the normal development of the child, the first signs of modesty appear about the age of 8 to 10 when the child has reached the point that he is aware of himself as an individual person. Then he begins to close the door when he goes into the bathroom and is sensitive about anyone else coming in. He wants to bathe by himself and dress alone. There is not much one can do to bring about this emerging sense of modesty any sooner; but when it does come, parents should respect the child's desire for privacy. The family may learn together that one knocks before one goes into a bathroom or bedroom. The child is now ready to be taught more fully what is considered proper and what is not: ladies keep their dresses down and their knees together; boys keep their pants zipped up and do not rub their crotch in public.

Of course modesty is a relative term, and in some matters what is "proper" is difficult to know. Some consider the bikini indecent, others do not. Whatever standard parents want their child to learn, they themselves must live by, so that their example agrees with their teaching. One little boy asked his mother as she was going out for the evening. "Where are you going, Mommie?" "To a concert, dear," she replied. The boy was worried and asked, "But won't somebody see you?" He was referring to her low cut dress and revealing a confusing inconsistency in the parents' teaching and practice.[6]

Modesty is taught by example. It is communicated through the attitude of parents. Parents who practice a "happy medium" in the home routine and dress are setting the foundation. This does not mean that a teen-ager will not dress immodestly at times in rebellion against modest parents. The power of the peer culture is very stong. If, however, the foundation has been well laid, it will continue to serve as a steadying guide through the years.

FOOTNOTES FOR CHAPTER III

1. Marion O. Lerrigo and Michael A. Cassidy, *Your Child from 9 to 12* (Chicago: Budlong Press Co., 1964), p. 25.
2. Dorothy Walter Baruch, *New Ways in Sex Education* (New York McGraw-Hill Book Company, Inc., 1959), pp. 15—16.
3. J. D. Ratcliff, "The Breast and Its Mysteries," *Reader's Digest*, LXXIX (October 1961), 54—56, as taken from *Family Doctor* (October 1961), published by the British Medical Association.
4. Ardis Whitman, "What Not to Tell a Child about Sex," *Redbook*, CXVI (January 1961), 42—44.
5. Deryck Calderwood, "Differences in the Sex Questions of Adolescent Boys and Girls," *Marriage and Family Living*, XXV, 4 (November 1963), 494.
6. Clyde M. Narramore, *How to Tell Your Children About Sex* (Grand Rapids: Zondervan Publishing House, 1950), p. 32.

IV.
Answering the First Questions (up to 5 years)

After the final session of a 6-hour sex education course, a father stepped forward to thank the instructor. As part of his thanks he confessed, "When the first big day finally came and my daughter asked, 'Where did I come from?' I was a complete blank."

Many fathers or mothers have the same difficulty. They know the facts. They know what they should tell their children, but somehow the questions don't seem the same as they are in the books. The impersonal book knowledge becomes very loaded with feeling when it is spoken to one as intimate as your own child. How different to look at the black print of an inanimate page than to look into the sparkling eyes of a questioning child! The personal relationship that exists between parents and child and the parents' own attitude make Christian conversation about sex a pleasant task or a very difficult one.

In the chapters that follow we shall offer some ways to get started. We offer these suggestions not to provide the only answers to questions, but to show how some people have done it and how one might begin.

In order to be better prepared to answer the needs of the child one should know what to expect of him at a given age level. For that purpose we include a section at the beginning of each of the chapters that follow on "Understanding the Age."

THE PRIMARY EMOTIONS

It is thought that the only feelings a small baby has are the feelings of pleasantness or unpleasantness.[1] He enjoys a warm, dry bed, a full stomach, and loving arms around him. He is irritated by a wet bottom and an empty stomach. These feelings or physical sensations of the body are the beginning of the emotions. They develop as the baby grows. After a time he learns to express dissatisfaction or anger when he has unpleasant sensations — pain, discomfort, or restriction of movement. This resentment is expressed with loud cries which parents soon recognize and are able to distinguish from cries of hunger. Anger is considered one of the primary or first emotions, together with fear and love. A child experiences fear when he hears an unexpected loud noise or when he is dropped suddenly. He has feelings of pleasant love when someone holds him firmly and gently, cuddles him and talks kindly to him, or sings to him. Later other emotions develop, such as jealousy, anxiety, and sympathy, but the foundation or basic emotions are anger, fear, and love. For the best development of these, one tries to encourage feelings of love and avoid situations which cause fear and give rise to anger. The child will be better able to handle feelings of anger and fear when he is first strengthened in love experiences, than if he at first knows more fear and anger than love.

PASSING THROUGH STAGES

When Ann learned to walk she often lost her pacifier, so her mother tied it on a string around her neck. When Grandmother saw it, however, she was horrified. "You'll ruin that child, letting her suck on that thing all the time. Her mouth will be deformed and she won't ever be able to talk right." But the mother wasn't disturbed. "She's still in the sucking stage, and she'll get over it when the time comes. If she doesn't, then I'll get concerned and we'll do something. Right now she has a need to suck, and I'm going to let her."

A wise mother indeed. A child in the first and second year has a need to suck. The mouth and the lips are the sensitive areas which, when stimulated, produce enjoyable sensations. And thank God they are! These sensations make a baby suck nipples and bottles through which he gets his food.

The child grows out of this stage when he is 2 or 3 years old. The attention in our culture then shifts to elimination control. The child begins to recognize the need to urinate or defecate in the toilet rather than in his diaper, and gradually he learns to control the necessary muscles. Of course, the switch from diaper to toilet doesn't operate like turning on a light switch. It is a slow learning process, and there is a great difference in the ages at which it is achieved. The various sensations in the bladder and rectum that are necessary for control must first develop, and trying to force a child before this time only causes frustration for both the parent and the child. Some children begin control at the age of 2, while others do not achieve it until 4 or 5.

It is also at this time that the child "discovers" his genitals and may play with them as he does with his toes or other parts of his body. He experiences a pleasant feeling, so he handles and manipulates them. Parents who know that this is normal need not become overly concerned, for this is a stage which will ordinarily pass.

The third stage comes between 3 and 6 years as the child becomes aware of being a boy or a girl. A boy identifies more closely with his father and a girl with her mother. Each may develop some feelings of competition with the same-sexed parent in a secret desire to marry the one of the other sex. Later the child realizes how impossible this is and comes to take the parent for a beloved model.

In this period a child learns to play with other children though he very much needs the security found in the assurance and certainty that his parents love him even when he ventures off to play with others. It is a big step from being a helpless infant to playing with peers!

A newborn baby is very self-centered. His first consciousness or awareness is of himself. He is concerned only with satisfying his own desires. Not until he has passed the first year is he ready to begin learning to give love by pleasing others. At 2 or 3 years he still needs to be the center of attention in the home and cannot, at this age, see another baby come into the home and share that attention without being affected. The new baby is an intruder, taking away some of the time and attention he has come to feel belong to him alone. Parents ought to prepare a child for this experience and expect some reaction to the change. Usually his feelings will fluctuate between moods of jealousy toward the baby and satisfaction in pleasing the parents. The youngster's great need is to be sure of his parents' continued love.

LEARNING TO KNOW GOD'S LOVE

The Sunday school teacher was telling her nursery class, "I know someone who is big and strong and cares for us. He loves us very much and is concerned about everything we do." "Oh, I know who that is," one boy chimed in. "That's my dad."

A small child's concept of God comes through his relationship to his parents. He understands God's love and care for him through the love of his parents or other adults who are close to him. In these important early years the feeling of being wanted and being sure of the love of those around him is the foundation upon which one's trust and confidence in God will be built. Some people believe that unless there is a satisfactory love relationship in these years one will never be able to love, either God or others, fully and completely. There is no question about God's love, but when one has not experienced love it is difficult to understand the abstract word "love."

A child at this age may become confused about the many concepts of God which surround him. He may have difficulty with the different names of God, Father, Jesus Christ, Holy Sprit. He may wonder: "What does God look like? How can that picture on the wall be Jesus when Mother said He is in heaven?" "My Sunday school teacher said Jesus is everywhere at the same time. Why can't I see Him?" This is a time when parents need patiently and lovingly to teach about God through the language of relationship and through simple Bible stories. This is the time a child begins to learn to talk to God in simple prayers and to be sure of His concern and love.

Questions About Differences in Sex

One of the first things that a child discovers as he becomes aware of his body is that not everyone is the same. Perhaps he sees a sister, or brother, or even a parent in the nude, and he wonders why he is different from them. Sometimes he may even worry about it. To have wholesome attitudes toward sex, one must feel right about his own sex without fears and worries about differences. To lay the foundation for these attitudes, questions about the differences in sex must be satisfied with correct information and good feelings. Christian parents seek to impart the main attitudes during the time of these early questions:

1. God made me the way I am, male or female.

2. I accept my own sex with thankfulness to God.

3. My parents are eager to answer my questions about sex. The following are sample answers to representative questions from this period. They should be used only as starters. Each parent will need to adapt them to his own way of conversing with his own child.

"WHAT'S THAT THING?"

"That's a penis. God made all boys with one. Boys pass their waste water (urine) through it. (This is called urination.)"

"WHY DO I HAVE A PENIS?" "WHY DOESN'T SISTER?"

"God made girls different from boys. They have an opening between their legs through which they urinate instead of through a penis. (This is called a urethra.) Boys have a penis and grow up to be fathers. Girls have a urethra and vagina and will grow up to be mothers."

55

"WHY IS MOTHER'S CHEST BIG AND SOFT?"

"God planned that as soon as babies are born they should have the kind of milk they need to make them grow. God makes this milk in Mother's breasts. Babies suck the nipple on the breast to get the milk. The breasts have to be big enough to store the milk. Because they are soft, the baby can rest his head when he drinks the milk. Some mothers don't have enough milk to feed their babies, or don't like to nurse them from their breasts, so they give them milk from a bottle."

"WHY DOES DADDY HAVE SO MUCH HAIR ON HIS CHEST?" "WHY DOES HE HAVE TO SHAVE?"

"As boys grow up they get hair in different places on their bodies. This shows that they are becoming men. Some dads have much more hair than others, depending on the family they come from. Because some of this hair grows on the face, men have to shave if they want a smooth face. God made women more smooth and beautiful with less hair growing on the body, and almost none on the face."

Questions About Where Babies Come From

When a child is 3 or 4 he begins to wonder where he came from. Sometimes this interest is stirred by the arrival of a brother or sister, a new baby in the neighborhood, offspring born to a pet, or sometimes even by a picture in a storybook.

Some children, however, never ask the question, "Where did I come from?" They know the answer before they need to ask the question. One home, for example, used the book *All About Eggs,*[2] which demonstrates with interesting and colorful pictures that babies come from eggs. It begins by showing how baby chicks, snakes, and other animals come from eggs we can see. It then shows how the eggs of other animals grow inside their mothers and how the baby is born when it is ready. The book concludes by illustrating how "you too grew inside your mother until you were ready to be born. . . ." The parents used this book

56

with their children already at the age of 2 for it held their interest and they wanted to hear it over and over. Thus they never did ask where they came from, for they knew. There are other fine books which do the same, and we especially recommend the first one in this series, *"I Wonder, I Wonder."*

In answering the questions which come in this general area, Christian parents should speak in a spirit of marvel and wonder at the way God causes babies to be made and to be born. They should show that they feel it a privilege to share with God in this miracle. The whole story cannot be told at this time. The child is not ready for it. He is limited by the stage of mental development he has reached. He wants a simple, direct, and honest answer to what his curiosity moves him to ask at this time.

"WHERE DID I COME FROM?"

"God made you. You grew in a warm, safe place inside your mother until you were big enough to live in the world, and then you came out."

"HOW DID I GET OUT OF YOU?"

"You grew in a 'baby place' inside your mother, called a uterus or a womb. When you were ready to be born, you came out through a special opening which God made between Mother's legs for babies to come out. This womb and the opening stretch, like a balloon stretches when there is air in it, but gets smaller again when the air is gone. That is why a woman who is going to have a baby (who is pregnant) gets big in front and then gets small again after the baby is born."

"HOW DID YOU FEED ME IN YOUR WOMB?"

"God arranged that in a marvelous way. He planned that, through a special tube from the mother to the baby, the baby could be fed from the mother's body. So mothers have to eat enough food to take care of two. When you were born, this tube was taken away and the place on your stomach where it was attached made a mark called your 'belly button' or navel."

"can i see where i came out?"

"You came out through a small opening between mother's legs. Women have one opening through which they pass waste water or urinate (urethra), another opening to pass waste when they have a bowel movement (anus), and a special opening through which the baby comes out (vagina). Usually we don't show these openings to other people except to someone like a doctor. The reason is that we believe it to be so precious and so private that it shouldn't be exposed for everybody to look at." (The parent may want to use a picture to show these openings.)

"do daddies have babies too?"

"No, God made the mothers to have the babies. But before a woman is able to have a baby she must have a man who can be the father. The father is to help care for the mother and the baby. Fathers are just as important as mothers, and they love their babies just as much as mothers do."

"will i be a mother (or father) someday?"

"If God wants you to be a mother, you will be. You will grow up and get married and have babies just as I did." (Some men and women decide not to get married when they grow up; and there are some who cannot have babies. They can adopt a baby, and it becomes just like their own.)

FOOTNOTES FOR CHAPTER IV

1. See books like: Armin Grams, *Children and Their Parents* (Minneapolis: T. S. Denison & Co., 1963).
2. Millicent Selsam, *All About Eggs and How They Change into Animals* (New York: William R. Scott, Inc., 1952).

V.
Answering the Questions
Of Childhood (ages 6—11)

Understanding the Age

In his book *Understanding Your Child,* Dr. James Hymes tells of having difficulty building a fence.[1] A neighbor who was watching finally spoke up. "Your nails are too big. That's why you split the wood. The wood can't take the size of nail you're using." He used thinner nails, and the wood did not split.

Something similar happens in child training when parents push a child to accomplishments before his rate of growth and development make him capable of achieving them. Each child develops at his own speed and is ready for learning new things at his own time along the way. The challenge is to know when is the right time, when the individual is ready so that the "nail will not split the wood."

"Understanding the Age" seeks to help by suggesting what to expect as the child grows from 6 to 11. Because this period covers many stages of rapid development, we cannot discuss them in detail. Here is a summary of the key changes:

HE HIDES HIS FEELINGS

The 6- or 7-year-old is growing up and is forced to shed some of his childish ways and expressions of emotion. This shows up when he shies away from sitting on his mother's lap, even though he may still want to do it. He feels that this is for small children and not for big ones! He may refuse to let mother kiss and coddle him, and he may hesitate to express his affection to her. With brazen abandon and bragging ways he tries to separate himself from any activities which might label him a baby.

HE ENJOYS THE SAME SEX

As the child continues to progress through this period, he more and more wants to be what he is, male or female, according to the pattern of the people among whom he lives. For a while after entering school, boys and girls pay little attention to the sex of their playmates. At 7 or 8 years, however, boys usually begin to prefer to play with boys and emphasize such masculine traits as courage, daring, and strength. They may form clubs or cliques and want nothing to do with those "sissy" girls. They roughhouse and wrestle. This preference for boys may continue through to the teen years.

Girls in the early preteen years also prefer to associate with their own sex and are interested in things their culture considers more feminine. Those girls who are more mature in this age group may begin to take an interest in boys and express it first by teasing and then by boy-girl friendships.

There are exceptions to these general patterns of development, however, which are determined largely by the individual development of the boys and girls and by the social customs of a given community.

As each child continues to mature, he wants to be less and less dependent on his parents. He seeks new ways of expressing himself unmolested by the adults who have watched him so closely until now. Parents often feel like one mother who said, "I see such changes in Cindy in just the last 6 months. She was always our cute little girl, but now that she is 10 she is rapidly growing out of the little girl stage. For the time being my husband and I almost feel that we are losing our little girl." [2]

At this age there develops in the child a unique curiosity which is a gift from God Himself. It is the incentive which leads him to ask "Why?" and becomes the basis for much interesting learning. It extends to everything, including sex. Before the 6th year, sexual interest is mainly in exploring one's own body, but at this age the interest turns to the bodies of others. The child becomes curious about how other children of both sexes look, and he needs to learn in one way or another. It is not unusual for children to go to the bathroom together and show each other their genitals and buttocks. Some play doctor or nurse and undress to examine each other. They may learn jokes about toilet functions and giggle when a word may be taken to refer to such things.

How can parents help during this age of curiosity? They may guide their child with firmness, gentleness, and patience. They may give direct information to satisfy curiosity in a way which shows respect for sex and communicates that the human body or the functions performed in the bathroom are not shameful. This interest is part of a natural curiosity. It must be accepted as such so that it can be discussed in a friendly framework. This is the way parents can help lead their child to wholesome attitudes.

HE NEEDS A SURE FAITH

After seeing a television report of a 13-year-old boy who had killed a 7-year-old girl, Jim asked his father, "Why did God let him do it? If God is so good, why does He let people be bad?"

Jan was helping her mother bake when her mother said, "Get the flyswatter and rid me of that pesky fly."

Jan hesitated and asked, "Why did God make flies anyway, Mother? They just bother people and carry so many germs. They aren't good for anything."

This is the type of question that is asked at this age about God. As the child finds answers to these questions his concepts mature and his faith grows. At the same time his conscience begins to sharpen and he becomes aware of personal sin. He ought to know by now the Gospel answer for sin, that he is God's child in Christ, that he is loved and forgiven. He needs this assurance especially at those times when he feels he doesn't deserve it.

During this period a child wants definite answers. Things are for him either black or white, right or wrong, and there isn't much room between.

The parents' own personal relationship to Jesus Christ and their own Christian convictions are very important here for parents are the models children imitate and the heroes many of them "worship."

Understanding some of the needs and characteristics of the child during this age will help parents answer questions and discuss problems in a sympathetic spirit.

The Father's Place

"But how do you tell them about sleeping with a woman in a simple, direct way without blushing?" a father asked in a question-and-answer period after a lecture on "How to Tell Your Children About Sex." He was almost blushing when he asked it. It was apparent that for him the subject was emotionally charged with embarrassment. The lecturer's answer began by suggesting that first he had to begin using the right words. He couldn't use the four-letter words that are picked up from the gang and he couldn't explain intercourse with terms like "sleeping with a woman."

To explain cohabitation and the father's place in the reproduction of children is very difficult because this is so far removed from the child's experiences and because the child is often not familiar enough with the anatomy of man and woman to make sense out of a direct answer. Yet without a correct understanding of procreation as the normal way in which husbands and wives show their love to each other and cooperate with the Almighty in the creation of children, a child cannot develop wholesome Christian attitudes toward sex. When speaking of the father's role it is important to point out the other equally vital roles of the father in loving his family and providing food and home. In this way the child is enabled to develop respect for persons and for the process of reproduction.

Books are helpful at this age, and parents may want to use the pictures or drawings in a good book to show the process of reproduction. The book in this series for this age is: *Wonderfully Made: What Preteens Want to Know.* Others are suggested in the back of this book. The questions below will in part be answered by these books, but we suggest one way of answering them with or without the aid of the books.

"WHAT MAKES THE BABY START GROWING INSIDE THE MOTHER?"

"God, of course, makes the baby grow. The father puts into the mother's body a tiny cell which joins with one from the mother. These two cells join together and begin to grow. The father's cell is called a sperm, and the mother's cell an egg or ovum. This is why a baby often looks like his mother or father, or a little like both, because both mother and father have a part in making the baby start. When a baby is growing inside a woman's uterus, we say that she is pregnant."

"HOW DOES THE FATHER PUT THE SPERM INTO THE MOTHER?"

"As the father's penis is placed into the mother's vagina, the sperm cells go from the penis into the mother's vagina to hunt for her egg cell. If one sperm finds the ovum and joins it, the baby starts growing. This is called 'mating' in animals. In people we call it sexual intercourse, physical or marital relations (cohabitation, copulation, or coitus)."

"DO I HAVE SPERM (EGGS) TOO?"

"Sperm cells are made by the testicles of a man. Small boys do not have sperm because their testicles (or testes) are not yet mature. When you get older, your penis grows bigger, your testicles develop, and then you have sperm cells.

"The egg cell or the ovum comes from the woman's ovaries,

63

which are two glands, one on each side of her body near the hip line. They are shaped like almond nuts. Each ovary contains about 30,000 eggs, and one of them is released each month when a woman is old enough to be a mother. You have these ovaries in your body now, and when you grow up they will begin to let an egg cell loose each month so you can become a mother."

"DOES KISSING MAKE YOU PREGNANT?"

"Kissing is a way in which a man and a woman show that they love each other, but it is not the same as intercourse. You cannot start a baby by kissing. Only through intercourse can the cells from the father and mother get together and start a baby."

"DO YOU HAVE A BABY EVERY TIME YOU SLEEP TOGETHER?"

"No! Mothers and fathers sleep together many times without having sexual relations, so the sperm and ovum cannot unite and start a baby. Even when they have intercourse, many times the sperm cells will not find an ovum and so no baby can be started."

"CAN I WATCH YOU HAVE INTERCOURSE?"

"Parents do not want anyone to see them have intercourse. How would you feel if I asked you to undress in the middle of the living room with the whole family watching? That's how married people feel about sexual relations. It is so private and personal that they would not feel right to have anyone watch them. When you grow up and learn to love someone very much, you will want to marry. And when you are married you and your wife (husband) will also want privacy while you have sexual relations." [3]

The Growing Baby

In his excellent book *Sex Attitudes in the Home*, Ralph Eckert tells the story of 5-year-old Janie, who watched the birth of a tiny coal-black kitten. She looked with shining eyes. "Midnight loves her kitten! She's just licking it all over!" Soon there were three little kittens. Sue, age 11, who was also watching, was lost in wonder after the weeks of waiting. "Midnight's purring. She's so happy. It's a miracle." [4]

In a similar way children are mystified at the birth of a baby and will ask many questions. Some questions about birth are difficult to answer and some seem to be irreverent or irrelevant. In the answers it is important to remember more than the mere facts. Children need the facts indeed. But the emotional impact that the answers have and the attitudes they build are more important. The goal of Christian parents is to give the correct information coupled with an attitude toward those facts that marvels at the mystery of life and stands in reverence before the Creator and Lord. Here are some of the questions which might be asked. When you don't know all the answers say, "I don't know, let's look it up."

"WHY DOES MOTHER GET SO BIG?"

"A baby starts to grow in the mother's uterus (or womb) when the father's sperm joins the mother's egg. When these two cells come together they make one new cell so small that you can't see it without a microscope. But it grows in the uterus and as it gets bigger and bigger it needs more and more room. The womb of the mother stretches to give it more room, like a rubber balloon expanding from the size of a pear to the size of a watermelon. This pushes out the mother's abdomen, and she becomes big in front. Some women used to be ashamed to be seen in public when they were big during pregnancy, but today it is somewhat different. Women feel more free to go in public places with their good-looking maternity dresses. It is a wonderful thing to have a baby growing inside you."

"CAN THE BABY GET HURT IF THE MOTHER FALLS?"

"If the mother falls too hard, the baby could get hurt. That's why a mother is so careful. But God arranged for the little bumps and jolts which come while Mother does her regular work. He planned for the baby to float in a sac of fluid. God thought of everything, didn't He?"

"HOW CAN THE BABY LIVE WITHOUT AIR AND FOOD?"

"Before a baby is born, it can live without breathing air with its lungs or eating with its mouth as we do. The baby gets food and oxygen from the mother's blood supply and then her blood stream also carries away the body waste, because the baby does not urinate or have a bowel movement. By a long tube of tissue the baby is attached to the special lining of the uterus which has been prepared for this. The tube extends from the baby where your navel is. It is called the umbilical cord. As soon as the baby is born, it must start breathing air and eating food as we do. Sometimes to help it start breathing, the doctor has to give it a good pat on its back."

"WHAT HAPPENS TO THE TUBE WHEN THE BABY IS BORN?"

"When the baby is born, the umbilical cord is no longer needed, so the doctor cuts it off and disposes of it together with the special lining of the uterus. Your navel (or belly button as some children call it) looks as it does because it healed that way after the doctor cut the cord. The navel has no purpose now except that it does remind us that this is where we were attached to our mothers before we were born."

"DOES IT HURT TO CUT THE TUBE?"

"No, it doesn't hurt the baby because there is no feeling in the cord, and it doesn't hurt the mother because the whole lining of the uterus comes out and is thrown away."

"DOES IT HURT TO HAVE A BABY?"

"Having a baby is difficult work for both the mother and the baby. It hurts the mother a little because the muscles of the uterus and vagina have to stretch to make the opening large enough for the baby to come out. At the hospital doctors and nurses help the mother and relieve some of the discomfort with medicine. Some women, by taking exercises and training the muscles of the body, can learn to relax in the kind of way which lessens the discomfort. But most mothers are so happy to have the baby that they soon forget labor in the joy of receiving this new bundle of life. Jesus mentioned this in John 16:21."

"HOW BIG IS A BABY WHEN IT IS BORN?"

"When a baby grows in the mother's uterus for the full 9 months, it usually weighs from 6 to 8 pounds and is about 20 inches long when it is born. If the baby is born before 9 months, it may be smaller and may need special care. Often the small baby will have to stay at the hospital until it is big enough to come home."

Menstruation

Menstruation used to be called "the curse" or "sick" days, and there were many strange superstitions and fears about what happened. Today we can more easily speak of "the period" or even use the word "menstruation" without shame or fear.

Some people feel it is the special responsibility of the mother to prepare her daughter for the time she begins menstruating. It does seem a little more natural for the mother to do this than the father, but the father may and ought to do it if for some reason the mother does not. In either case girls should be prepared about the time they become 10, because the first period usually comes between 10 and 13, although a few cases come as early as 9 or as late as 14 and 15. Mothers ought not use their own beginning age as the absolute guide, for the age of the initial menstruation has dropped so that a daughter may begin to menstruate at an earlier age than her mother did.[5]

If a girl is not prepared for her first menstruation, the experience might frighten her and even cause her to feel guilty so that she will not ask questions about it. Mothers should plan opportunities to discuss it by letting their daughters see a box of sanitary napkins, or speaking of "mother's period."

Much help is provided in this area, perhaps more than in any other of sex education. Often the school or community organizations show a movie about menstruation and have a nurse present to answer questions about it. Every girl ought to have a chance to see such a movie. There are also booklets available from the sanitary napkin companies and a fine help is available in the book in this series: *Wonderfully Made: What Preteens Want to Know.*

We here suggest some approaches for personal discussions:

WHAT HAPPENS WHEN A GIRL MENSTRUATES?

"This refers to a flow of tissue and blood from the woman's uterus. Each month the woman's body is prepared for the beginning of a baby. Her ovaries release an egg cell. Her uterus grows a special spongy lining of glandular cells which form something of a nest for the fertilized egg. But if no male sperm joins the mother's egg, the special nest of cells is cleaned away. This material flows out of the uterus through the vagina. This happens about every 26–32 days. It lasts from 4 to 6 days and is sometimes called a woman's "period." The first periods come irregularly and often the flow is light. It may even be a year or so before a regular pattern is established."

"CAN A GIRL PLAY BALL DURING HER PERIOD?"

"Yes. You need to learn, of course, how to wear a sanitary napkin to keep your clothes from being soiled, but most girls can go about their usual activities. Some doctors impose no activity restrictions whatever; others suggest that strenuous activities like swimming, tennis, or bicycle riding be engaged in moderately. You will want to bathe or shower daily to help you feel fresh and clean and prevent unpleasant odors." [6]

"Many girls feel as well during their periods as at any other time, while some may feel a little headache, backache, or a few cramps, usually on the first day. A good thing to do if you feel this way is to take an aspirin and rest. The most common complaint girls have seems to be feeling down in the dumps just before and during the early part of their period. This feeling may be caused by changes taking place in the body, but some doctors suspect that it happens because girls think they should feel that way when they menstruate. Once in a while a girl does have real pain with menstruation. She should see her doctor." [7]

"DO ALL WOMEN MENSTRUATE?"

"All women menstruate until they are about 45–50 years old, at which time they experience what is called the 'change of life' or the 'menopause.' The woman's body no longer releases an egg cell each month after this, and the uterus stops providing the special lining for a baby, so there is no menstruation. This too is a part of God's wise plan. Because of this an older woman may still enjoy intercourse with her husband but not have any babies. After a woman is 50 years old she would have difficulty taking care of a baby until he grew up.

"A woman also does not menstruate during the time that a baby is growing in her womb. A short while after the baby is born she starts menstruating again and is able to have another baby."

"DO BOYS HAVE SOMETHING LIKE MENSTRUATION?"

"Only women can be mothers, so only women menstruate. Boys or men have nothing exactly like it, but God designed a way in which their bodies pass off the unused sperm cells. These pass off through the penis in a white fluid." (See the section on seminal emissions in the next chapter.)

General Questions

There is no way of knowing all the questions that a child will ask, nor is it possible to know in what manner he will ask them. There are many areas of sex education which ought to be discussed during this stage. If the child does not ask questions about them, parents may need to take the initiative to bring them up for conversation. We have chosen a few typical questions. Parents must go on from here and discuss the needs of their child in their own way.

"WHY DO MEN ATTACK GIRLS?"

"Some girls are attacked by men who are sick in their minds. They have something in them that makes them want to see a naked girl, play with their bodies, torture them, or have intercourse with them. You can't tell who these people are, so you have to be careful about the strangers you meet."

"WHAT SHOULD I DO WHEN A STRANGER TALKS TO ME?"

"Be polite and friendly to all strangers but never take candy or gifts or get in a car with one. If anyone tries to touch you on the bus or in a movie, move to a different seat, and if he keeps bothering you tell the driver or an usher or the manager. It's always best to go places like a theater with another friend or, if you are going out after dark, to walk with another person. If you see a man following you or hanging around school, or if anything else unusual happens, tell me or your teacher about it."

"WHAT IS A VIRGIN?"

"A virgin is a woman who has never had intercourse with a man or a man who has never had intercourse with a woman. You are a virgin."

A child may also ask about words which he hears or reads, like rape, adultery, homosexuality, and so forth. The glossary in the back of this book will help you understand them.

Masturbation

A Christian mother, very concerned and worried about her 5-year-old daughter, described her actions like this: "I catch her in the bathroom working with her vagina by rubbing and washing it until a satisfied feeling comes. She seems to act like an adult."

FACTS TO REMEMBER

Why does a boy or girl masturbate at this age? Not because he has any sensual desires or lusts, but because he enjoys it. He handles his genitals and feels a pleasing sensation, so he repeats it. This is not uncommon between 2 and 6. Parents may have to talk to their child about it so that it does not develop into a serious habit. Usually, however, he outgrows this sex play so that only in rare cases does it become a problem.

The counselor to whom the mother mentioned above presented her problem suggested that she begin with these two things: (1) Take the daughter to a doctor for a physical examination to see if anything were causing excessive irritation or stimulation; (2) Plan activities with the girl to keep her occupied and her mind away from the habit.

The next period in which a child may handle his genitals is between the ages of 12 and 20. By this time a boy has matured enough to have ejaculation of seminal fluid and to derive more pleasure from manipulating the sexual organs. There is no easy answer for what parents should do if they discover a child masturbating at this age, because many boys and some girls masturbate as a part of their experimentation and growth in searching for an expression of their sex urge. However, "some medical authorities now regard masturbation as a step in preparation for adult sexual feelings." [8]

Masturbation was formerly called "self-abuse." Children were told that masturbation would be harmful physically and mentally — like making one lose his mind, give him acne, ulcers, or tuberculosis. Today modern medical science assures us that masturbation does not cause any bodily harm and that most young people overcome the habit as they grow older.

Masturbation is essentially an immature form of sexual behavior. While most young people rather quickly grow out of this stage, to persist in this activity is to persist in what is an inherently selfish form of sexual behavior. Out of fear or lack of understanding, parents sometimes are too severe in their discipline, with the result that the masturbator comes to look on himself as an especially dirty sinner and inferior to his brothers and sisters, playmates and schoolmates. All of us have need for confession of the sin of selfishness, and the masturbator should not be singled out as a *special* sinner.

SUGGESTIONS FOR CONVERSATION

Knowing the facts about masturbation will help to temper any treatment or discussion, and it is important to avoid harsh treatment, ridicule, or criticism. A teen-ager develops the habit of masturbation because of the enjoyment he gets from the act or because he is compensating for a lack in his personality makeup. He may use masturbation as a release from excessive tension or fear, such as fear of failure or rejection. Masturbation is often found in children who are concerned about the relations of their parents to one another or their own relationship to their parents. It is often the shy youngster who masturbates, the one who does not make friends easily and who wants to be by himself more than with the gang.

Some people use the motive of fear and guilt to try to control the habit of masturbation, pointing out how God will punish it. But this is certainly not the Christian approach. Neither is it very successful. Most young people want to control the habit for it is often accompanied by a sense of shame and guilt. Dr. Lerrigo says, "Parents can help most when they refrain from adding to such feelings, and when they create a happy, relaxed home life with ample opportunities for their child to enjoy healthy, absorbing, and interesting pursuits." [9]

Christian parents ought to use the love of God as motive rather than fear of His punishment. When Christ lives in us we have His power to help us control our lives. Understanding that it may be some lack in the teen-ager's life that causes him to masturbate, parents may help by guiding him in finding friends and companions, discovering ways of obtaining satisfaction from activities he enjoys, assuring him of their genuine love, or doing things with the family and with others. As they discuss the problem they should encourage the adolescent to make his own decision to break the habit with the help of God and, above all, lead him to pray to God for help and guidance and for freedom from this form of sexual selfishness.

If nothing can be accomplished in this way, then, of course, the final step is to seek the professional help of a psychiatrist.

FOOTNOTES FOR CHAPTER V

1. James L. Hymes, Jr., *Understanding Your Child* (New York: Prentice-Hall, Inc., 1952), p. 11.

2. Lorenz F. Weber, "Boy Sprouts and Girl Sprouts," *The Growing Child,* Parents Guidance Series No. 11 (St. Louis: Concordia Publishing House), p. 26.

3. Ralph G. Eckert, *Sex Attitudes in the Home* (New York: Popular Library, 1956), p. 31.

4. Ibid., p. 53

5. Marion O. Lerrigo and Michael A. Cassidy, *Your Child from 9 to 12* (Chicago: Budlong Press Company, 1964), p. 4, quoting from C. A. Mills, "Geographic and Time Variations in Body Growth and Age of Menarche," *Human Biology* (September 1937), pp. 43—56, points out that at the end of the 18th century the average age at the first menstruation was about 16½ years. The change is attributed by some scientists to higher nutritional standards in our modern diet, particularly to the high level of protein it contains.

6. Marion O. Lerrigo and Michael A. Cassidy, *A Doctor Talks to 9 to 12 year olds* (Chicago: Budlong Press Company, 1964), pp. 60—62.

7. Ibid., p. 80

8. Marion O. Lerrigo and Michael A. Cassidy, *Your Child from 9 to 12* (Chicago: Budlong Press Company, 1964), p. 6.

9. Ibid.

VI.
Answering the Questions
Of the Junior High Age
(ages 12 – 14)

Understanding the Age

The boys in one junior high school were catching the girls in the hallway and feeling their breasts. When the principal found out about it, he called them in and asked why they did it. The answer was simple, "We wanted to see if they were real or if they were wearing falsies."

This is the kind of behavior that one might expect from some junior high boys, and to them this did not seem dirty or promiscuous, only mischievous. We might summarize this age with these points:

SEX ORGANS AND CHARACTERISTICS ARE MATURING

This is the age of rapid physical growth. Girls may begin their growth spurt as early as 11 years and often reach their full height by 14, as compared to boys, who have their rapid growth between 13 and 14 and often reach their full height by 16. The adolescent boy or girl may grow 3 to 4 inches a year and gain from 10 to 20 pounds. These physical changes are sparked by hormones of the pituitary glands located at the base of the brain. One of these hormones also stimulates the sex glands to develop and mature.

The sex organs develop together with the total body in this period of rapid growth, and of course boys and girls become conscious of this. Hair begins to grow on the face, in the pubic region, and under the arms. The girls are beginning to broaden in the hips and develop the curves of the female figure. Their breasts are developing and they begin to wear brassieres. Boys note these changes in the girls' figures and are curious, although at this age they usually have no real interest in sexual activity. At times they are attracted to girls but do not know how to show their interest or still think of it as being sissy. So boys tend to develop the kind of aggressive behavior which involves teasing and general showing off in front of girls.

Girls at this age mature faster than boys and are ahead of them until they are about 15, when the boys begin to catch up again. But at the junior high level the girls may often be as tall or taller than the boys and be more mature. This is why junior high girls often think boys of their age are silly and get crushes on older boys or men.

CONFLICT WITH PARENTS

"But, Mother, everybody is wearing heels! I can't go to the party in those kid shoes!" Jane argued until her mother wore down and gave in. Most parents of junior high youngsters have gone through similar experiences, for at this age conflicts with parents grow more distinct and numerous than in the previous years. The teen-ager is powerfully influenced by the group of boys and girls with whom he associates, and he wants to be like them and live like them. Parents need a new measure of patience and understanding to cope with this phenomenon so they may help their child through this age in a way which prepares for even deeper conflicts in the older-teen years.

This is the time also to learn new ways and techniques of handling differences, so that the door is kept open for continuing guidance. As the junior high youngster develops his sex characteristics, he is also developing new feelings and emotions. These make him act in different and strange ways, which at times shock and bewilder parents.

After Jim has been respectful and obedient during the years of 10 and 11, Father is puzzled and shocked to see the reaction when he refused to let Jim go swimming one afternoon. Jim shouts, "All right, pick on me. I don't care!" He runs to his room, slams the door, and throws himself on the bed. What should Dad do? Go into the room and try to explain? Should he give in? Should he punish him for this kind of "sassy" rebellion? Or should he just let Jim struggle through by himself? The last seems to be the best course of action. Jim is experiencing new emotions as he grows up and he must learn how to handle them. He needs, of course, also to know that his father is concerned about him and willing to talk to him, but that he will not be influenced by rebellion. Gradually Jim must develop self-discipline and a sense of responsibility. Dad cannot command and dictate every action but must learn to trust Jim more and more to make his own decisions. Dad has to learn to stand by his side and to guide and suggest.

FAITH NEEDED TO REMOVE EXCESSIVE FEELINGS OF GUILT

Every age has its own special temptations and vulnerable spots. For the junior high youngster the Achilles heel seems to be feelings of guilt. When a boy in this age has his first "wet dream" without having been prepared for it, he may worry that God is punishing him for the sex drive which he has felt, for his sexual experimentation, or the manipulation of his penis. He may think he is bad and sinful and yet be afraid to talk to anyone about it. How can he admit that he has played with himself or looked at a "dirty" book? This is how excessive feelings of guilt develop at his age.

There are many other ways in which a similar thing happens, of course. A girl, for instance, may develop guilt feelings over menstruation or the development of her breasts. Her breasts are not as full as those of the other girls, so there must be a reason, she thinks. One reason she imagines is that God is punishing her. Or she may manipulate or rub her breasts in an attempt to make them bigger, and she feels guilty about this. Or a junior high girl may go out on a date and let a boy "neck" or "pet" or kiss her good night. She wonders whether this is all right or whether it is sinful to let a boy kiss her or touch her breasts.

There are many similar perplexing questions. Unless the junior high youngster is guided to adequate answers which help him cope with the various situations and problems he faces, he will develop feelings of guilt and shame, of uncertainty and confusion. He needs help to see the facts of physical development as a natural part of maturing into adulthood and preparing for parenthood. As his body matures and he becomes conscious of his drives, he must be led to feel that God's sustaining hand is at work. He does not have to be ashamed of his body. It is the good gift of a loving God.

To help him achieve this attitude is the task of the parent and all who work with the junior high boy or girl — the teacher, the Sunday school teacher, the pastor, and others. The example and guidance of these people should assist him to accept himself and his body, to feel right with God, to control his actions, and to handle his feelings.

When in his experimentation the junior high youngster does things which are not right and he feels are not right, he needs to be told that in God's sight they are not right but he must also be given the assurance of the love and forgiveness of God. He will appreciate an opportunity to talk with an understanding person about his feelings of guilt and penitence. Here is an excellent opportunity to assure him that God loves him not just when he is "good" but also when he is "bad." Parents may help by standing by with their love and forgiveness, by being more ready to understand than to scold, to listen than to judge, to forgive than condemn. Christian parents must demonstrate in their dealings with their teen-ager how God is constantly dealing with us in love and grace.

The Body Develops

Roberta is pleased about her developing breasts and wants to get a brassiere. "Yes, I'll go ask Mom," she says, as she poses, chest thrust forward in front of her mirror. "I've got to have a bra to keep them set when I wear a sweater." But crestfallen she adds, "Mom said my clothes allowance was all used up."

"Oh!" says her younger sister, "If Mommie won't buy you a bra, I've got some Band-Aids that would do." [1]

Most teen-agers worry about the changes that take place in their bodies as they mature. A girl may be pleased, as Roberta, when her breasts begin to develop, for now she can have a figure like the older set. But there are many problems. She may worry not only about getting her bra, but whether her breasts will develop to average size, or be larger or smaller. As she learns about intercourse, she may wonder whether a penis will fit into her vagina or whether it will hurt. A boy may be concerned about the size of his penis. Is it smaller than those of other boys? Will he be able to have normal relations with a woman? Can he be a father?

Such questions, unless properly answered, will cause fears and anxieties. Many adolescents find it difficult to come to their parents with these concerns, especially if they have not been doing so in the years before this age. If it is possible for parents to initiate frank discussions, they may be able to lead the boy or girl to express what is bothering them. Here are some "starter" answers to questions which may give parents some ideas how to talk with their child.

"WHY DOES MY PENIS GET HARD?"

"Blood fills up the spongy tissue of the penis so that it becomes erect. At times your penis may be hard when you wake up in the morning, but this is because the bladder is full of urine. This causes pressure which stimulates some nerves so that an erection occurs. There are also other things which cause erection. Scientists have enumerated 40 different causes, such as tight clothes, riding a bicycle, handling the penis, looking at pictures of nudes, and many more. If your penis erects, just ignore it and in a little while it will go back to normal."

"WHAT IS CIRCUMCISION?"

"Circumcision is a small operation to cut away the loose skin (foreskin) over the end of the penis. If this is not done, waste material called smegma accumulates under the foreskin and needs to be washed away regularly. It is the custom among Jews that all boy babies are circumcised when they are 8 days old. Many other baby boys are also circumcised in our time, because this makes it easier to keep the penis clean."

"WHAT ARE THOSE 'RUBBERS' YOU GET IN THE RESTROOMS AT THE SERVICE STATIONS?"

"The proper name for it is condom. It is a thin rubber sack made to slip over the penis and wear during intercourse. The advertisements say that they are to be used to keep from spreading diseases of the sex organs, but most people use them to prevent the start of a baby as the result of their relations. The male sperm is caught in the sack so that it cannot enter the woman's uterus and join the egg to start a baby. Some teen-agers think that by using condoms for intercourse before they are married, it is all right because it is 'safe.' For a Christian, however, 'safe' doesn't make it right. For him intercourse, as God designed it, is part of the love surrender in marriage. To engage in it before marriage is a sin called fornication."

"WILL MY BREASTS GET BIGGER IF I RUB THEM?"

"Some people think that if you rub or play with your breasts they will get larger, but this isn't true. They will grow as big as they are supposed to grow no matter what you do or don't do to them. Just give them time to develop and then accept them as God made them."

"IS IT ALL RIGHT TO WEAR FALSIES?"

"There is no need to wear falsies just as there is no need to wear a wig over your hair, or an extension over your arm, unless there is something physically wrong. We accept our bodies as

God made them and are thankful if they are healthy. Perhaps we need to ask why we want to wear them? A little padding because of social pressure is different than trying to be 'sexy.' If a woman has a deformity or has a breast removed in an operation, of course, this is different."

"DOES EVERYONE GET HAIR BETWEEN HIS LEGS?"

"Yes, everyone gets some 'pubic hair,' as it is called, as well as hair under the arms. Men also get hair on their chest and face. This hair is a sign that we are maturing sexually."

Seminal Emissions

"Mature" is a relative word. When we speak of a boy maturing in his intellect, character, or personality, no one can set a time as to when it is accomplished. But when it comes to being sexually mature a time is usually set — when a boy has his first ejaculation of semen. This could come through masturbation or through seminal emission. It usually happens around the age of 14, although it could vary a year or more either way.

While ejaculation is accompanied by pleasurable sensations, the experience may be frightening if it occurs in a seminal emission before the boy understands what is happening. Before he reaches 13, he should know what to expect and what to do when it happens. The father is probably better suited to explain it to him than the mother.

If a child does not hear about nocturnal emission in the colloquial expression of "wet dream," or does not read about it in a book, he may never ask about it until it happens and then he may be too ashamed or full of guilt to bring it up. A way should be found to discuss the matter in order to raise these two basic questions:

"WHAT HAPPENS IN A 'WET DREAM'?"

"A wet dream is a normal experience for boys whose sex organs are mature enough to have intercourse. Semen, which the testes have made, accumulates and during sleep is discharged through the penis. That is why the right expression is seminal emission, or nocturnal emission, since it happens during one's sleep at night. The name 'wet dream' is popular since it is an easier expression to learn and remember and the experience is frequently associated with dreams about girls or sex play."

"WHAT SHOULD I DO WHEN IT HAPPENS?"

"Seminal emissions just happen as part of God's way of taking care of accumulated semen, and there is no way of knowing when it will happen or how often. In fact you may never have a wet dream or you may have many of them. Usually they stop after you are married and use the semen during regular intercourse.

"When it happens, all you need do is wash up, get a clean pair of pajamas, and go back to sleep. Don't worry about the stains on the sheets. Mother will understand."

Sexual Intercourse

By this age children will usually know what sexual intercourse is, even though their parents may never have talked to them about it. Recent studies indicate that one third to one half of boys and girls name friends of their own age as their chief source of sex information.[2]

In the average community and home it must be assumed that the junior high youngster knows something about what constitutes sexual relations. If his chief source of information has been his friends, his facts may be twisted and his feelings confused. He may be curious about details and wonder if what he has been told is really true. Parents may have to explain patiently and even repeat some things which were already discussed at an earlier age, when he didn't fully absorb them.

Some of the questions might be:

"Sometimes this 'making love' refers only to going out on dates, while at other times it may refer to kissing and petting. Sometimes it is also used to refer to sexual relations. Whenever you love someone, it is always exciting. In marriage intercourse has a special thrill. It is the highest expression of physical love for a husband and wife to possess each other so completely. The climax for the man comes with a high level of pleasing feeling as the penis ejects a whitish fluid called semen which carries the male sperm. The pleasure of the woman varies. Some women have a climax or orgasm similar to men, only without the ejection of semen. Other women have a more general feeling of excitement which makes them feel good all over.

"This 'making love' is a normal and natural part of the marriage relationship in which husband and wife give their bodies to each other in love."

"DOES A BABY START EVERY TIME YOU HAVE INTERCOURSE?"

"Not every intercourse produces a baby because in the delicate system which God designed there must be a female egg in the woman's tubes at just the right time for the male sperm to fertilize it. The egg which the woman's ovaries release once a month lives only a day or two, and so if the sperm does not enter it, it dies. The sperm lives about the same length of time before it too dies. No one can tell whether fertilization will happen until it does. With some women fertilization happens very readily and with others not so readily. Of course, there are ways of preventing fertilization. They are called 'birth control.'" (See the section on this in the next chapter.)

"HOW DOES HUMAN REPRODUCTION DIFFER FROM THAT OF ANIMALS?"

"Animals breed at a time when the egg in the female is ready to be fertilized. We say she is 'in heat.' At other times animals have no physical relations similar to intercourse among humans. Human beings may be ready for physical relations at any time. This is one way God made sex in people different from sex in animals. Sexual relations are a part of the surrender of love and can be enjoyed even when the woman's egg is not ready to be fertilized."

"COULD I HAVE INTERCOURSE?"

"You probably could since your body is just about mature enough, but it would not be the way that is right. Your body must still grow and your mind and spirit develop so that you can learn to love someone enough to want to live with him the rest of your life. Then you may marry and are ready for intercourse. To use outside of marriage what God created to be used only in marriage is a wrong use of God's creation and a sin against God."

"HOW COME JANE HAS A BABY AND SHE'S NOT MARRIED?"

"Sometimes people go against God's plan and will have marital relations without being married. If they have a baby this way, the baby has a real handicap because the father will not live with the mother and the baby, nor make the kind of home and family life that a baby needs."

"WHY DOES MOTHER GET SICK IN THE MORNING WHEN SHE'S GOING TO HAVE A BABY?"

"This is the way the bodies of some women react as they make the necessary changes to take care of the baby growing in their uterus. It is called 'morning sickness.' A doctor can usually help it with medicine. Some women are not ill at all and feel very well during the entire pregnancy."

"HOW IS THE BABY BORN?"

"A baby is ready to be born about 9 months after fertilization. He has grown enough to live in the outside world. His lungs are ready for breathing, his nerves and muscles work well together, his body is ready to receive and digest food. It's about time, too, for he has grown so big that his mother's uterus won't stretch much more to accommodate him.

"A mother knows when the birth is starting, when she feels the muscle contractions beginning. The muscles of the uterus begin to push the baby down, usually head first, into the vagina and then into the outside world. It takes hours, usually, for the muscles to stretch and expand and push the baby out.

"The mother goes to the hospital for this 'labor' because the doctor and nurses can help her and take care of the baby when it is born."

Heredity

Junior high youngsters are at an age when they love babies and enjoy playing with them. They marvel at the tiny creatures and ask questions about how they came to be the way they are. To answer these questions parents need some understanding of how children inherit certain characteristics from their families. Here is a simple brief explanation to some basic questions:

"WHY DO SOME CHILDREN LOOK LIKE THEIR PARENTS?"

"The male sperm and female ovum have in their centers 23 little threadlike objects of different shapes called chromosomes, which join together in the fertilized egg to make a total of 23 pairs, or a total of 46. Each of these chromosome threads has thousands of smaller beadlike substances called 'genes,' and it is through these genes that we inherit our likenesses to our parents or our grandparents. The genes decide whether the baby will have black or red, straight or wavy hair, blue or brown eyes, long or short legs, and so forth. Since 23 of the 46 chromosomes come from each parent, the child will look like either parent and inherit characteristics from both, depending on which of the genes are the 'dominant' ones. The story goes back even further than that. The father's chromosomes and genes came from both sides of his family, and the mother's from both sides of her family. Mother and father, therefore, pass on to their child chromosomes and genes from all four of their parents — and so on back for generations. Scientists can tell us many more fascinating things about the inheritance of traits, and they are learning more all the time. It all makes us marvel in amazement."

"WHAT DECIDES WHETHER THE BABY WILL BE A BOY OR A GIRL?"

"When the male sperm and the female ovum join in fertilization, they match up their chromosomes. One set of these determines whether the child will be male or female. The ovum has a chromosome called "X," but there are two kinds of sperms, an "X" sperm and a "Y" sperm. If an "X" sperm unites with the egg, it is a girl. If a "Y" sperm fertilizes the ovum, it is a boy. God has given us no control over this process, but it averages out to approximately 106 baby boys born for every 100 baby girls. There are probably more "Y" sperm that "X" sperm. There is no way of knowing what sex the baby will be until he is born, although the time may come when doctors can accurately use tests to determine this during pregnancy."

"WHAT CAUSES TWINS?"

"If a fertilized egg divides into two separate parts, then each part will develop into a baby. Since each part has the same chromosomes and genes, the babies will be *identical* twins, which means they look alike and are always both of the same sex. Sometimes twins are of different sex and do not look alike. We call these *fraternal* twins. In the case of fraternal twins, the mother has released two eggs and a different male sperm has fertilized each of them. Each sperm and each ovum has a different arrangement of chromosomes and genes, so the babies are as different as any ordinary brother and sister. Multiple births of more than two babies can happen either from one ovum or from separate ones, so triplets, quads, and quints can be either identical or fraternal, or a combination."

"Birthmarks are skin blemishes which are caused by the concentration of blood vessels or skin coloring (pigment) in one spot. They don't hurt or cause any harm, but are usually not very pretty, and if they are on the face or arms some people become self-conscious or even embarrassed about them. Some birthmarks can be removed with minor surgery. Otherwise one must learn to accept them and live with them as one of those unexplainable things that happen."

Dating

"I'll let you go to high school and send you to college, too," said one father some 25 years ago to his son who was graduating from the 8th grade, "but," he went on, "you've got to promise me one thing."

"What's that?" the eager youngster asked.

"Don't smoke or go out with girls until you are 21."

To a 13-year-old boy that didn't sound difficult. He had no interest in girls and hadn't even thought about smoking yet. So he made the promise. Within 2 years he had broken both promises without the father's knowledge and had to live for years with a guilty conscience.

Some 25 years ago the reaction of many parents to the dating of their teen-agers, especially their daughters, was one of resistance. Promises were exacted, rules were made, and many were forbidden their first date until 16 or 18 years old. While some parents react in a similar way today, the more common reaction is one of encouraging their children to date, even before they become teen-agers. Parents send their boys and girls to dancing school and during junior high promote social affairs to which their children go as couples.

Somewhere in discussion with the church and community and the teen-ager, parents must find a happy middle ground. Dating has a real purpose in the social and sexual development of boys and girls. Parents ought to prepare their teen-ager for dating by discussing its many aspects, striving to keep the channels open for continued frank conversation. To start thinking about the questions which are vital to this area, think of these:

"WHEN CAN I GO STEADY?"

"I can't make any rules for you about this. A lot depends on when you are ready for it. As you start dating you should meet different boys (or girls) and learn to get along with them. Then when you are ready to pick one with whom you want to go steady and perhaps marry one day, you will have a broader basis by which to choose. It's not very wise to take as a steady the first boy (or girl) that comes along, even though it's kind of nice to be sure you will always have a date. By going steady too young you are really cheating yourself out of friendships and dates with other boys (or girls)."

"IS IT ALL RIGHT TO LET A BOY KISS ME?"

"That depends on the kind of kissing and where it is done. There is nothing wrong with a boy kissing you good night in appreciation for the date or to show he likes you. But when you sit in a parked car or on the living room sofa and continue to kiss over and over, this leads to petting and caressing which could excite you or the boy, or both of you, and tempt you to go 'too far.' When your sexual desires are aroused, it sometimes makes you lose all sense of right and wrong and you have little control over yourself. Heavy petting and kissing are really a part of the preparation for sexual intercourse which should be reserved for marriage."

"WHAT DO YOU DO WHEN BOYS GET 'FRESH'?"

"After you have held hands and kissed for a while, a boy may next try to put his hands on your breasts and rub and squeeze them. He may place his hand on your knees or rub your thighs. He may try to reach your vulva and place his fingers into your vagina. This is a sure sign that he is trying to arouse you sexually. If you allow him to continue such sex play it may stir within you a strong excitement which causes you to lose control of yourself. There is nothing inherently evil in these feelings; they are part of the beautiful love relationship of husband and wife as they enjoy each other's bodies in marital relations. But you are not married. So when you become sexually aroused you either have to stop when your emotions are at a high pitch or you go on to intercourse, which, outside of marriage, violates the purpose of sex and is in violation of God's law and love and contrary, therefore, to your Christian standards. When a boy begins to feel you, it is good gently to put his hand away and say, 'No, please.' A Christian boy will respect you for it. If he does not accept your 'no' politely, ask him to take you home at once."

General Questions

"Is it all right to hold hands in church?" "Is it all right to dance with a boy that you don't know?" There is no end to the questions that fill the mind of the junior high youngster as he grows in his understanding of sex and begins to feel the stir of sexual drives within himself. It is impossible for a book to discuss an answer to every question, for there is no way of knowing what all the questions will be. Some questions which might be asked are these:

"WHAT DOES IT MEAN TO GET RAPED?"

"When a man forces a woman to have intercourse with him, this is called rape. There is usually something wrong with a man who does this. He may be sick mentally or his sexual desires and drives run out of control. He sees a woman and gets so stirred up that he will do anything, even hurt or kill, in order to have relations with her."

"CAN YOU GET PREGNANT IF YOU ARE RAPED?"

"Yes, you can. To get pregnant from intercourse, the female's egg and the male's sperm must meet and join. If this happens as a result of being raped, a woman becomes pregnant. If an unmarried girl gets pregnant from being raped, she often lets the baby be adopted by a couple who want a baby. Some people believe that when a young girl is raped it is all right to let the doctor remove the fertilized egg before it grows into a baby. If this is done, the girl will have had an abortion."

"WHAT IS ABORTION?"

"Abortion is an operation in which the embryo or fetus is removed from the womb of the mother before it is capable of living outside the uterus. It is illegal in the United States and in most countries unless two or more doctors agree that it is necessary for the health of the mother. There is no easy answer for every situation, but many Christians believe that an abortion not judged necessary to save the life of the expectant mother is the taking of a life. Today the church is facing the question of whether an abortion should be permitted in other situations. Sometimes the embryo or fetus is discharged by natural process from the uterus. This is called spontaneous abortion."

"WHAT IS ADULTERY (FORNICATION)?"

"When a married man has intercourse with a woman other than his wife, or a married woman has intercourse with another man, this is called adultery. The Bible also uses the word 'fornication' to refer to adultery, although fornication also means intercourse between those who are not married at all. This is one of the devil's temptations to destroy happy marriages and happy homes. Christian couples too must always be on their guard against these temptations."

A man or woman may love his partner very much but still fall victim to unfaithfulness. When a man is sure of the love and concern of his spouse and is enjoying satisfactory sexual relations with her, he is not as inclined to look toward another woman. The same is true for the wife, of course. When one falls, the other in a way shares in the failure. The Christian husband and wife will in repentance seek forgiveness for their failure. In

Christian love each partner must forgive the other, accept the fallen back, and try to strengthen the marriage lest it end in divorce.

FOOTNOTES FOR CHAPTER VI

1. Dorothy Walter Baruch, *New Ways in Sex Education* (New York: McGraw-Hill Company, Inc., 1959), p. 200.
2. Evelyn Millis Duvall, *Love and the Facts of Life* (New York: Association Press, 1963), p. 82.

VII.
Answering the Questions
Of the Senior High
And Young Adult

Understanding the Age

"I can't understand it. It just doesn't make sense. I can understand when they explain how we send a rocket to Mars or to the moon," Mr. Andrew rattled on in his complaint to his wife. "They can draw pictures and show me why it works the way it does. But these teen-agers nobody can explain! You'd think that after all the running around that's been going on the past week they would want to stay home and get some sleep. Instead they want to go to an all-night party."

Sounds like Mr. Andrew was having problems with the teen-agers in his family. Well, most parents do. And most teen-agers have problems with their parents too. Audrey Williamson suggests that "it is probable that the adolescent who is entirely satisfactory to his parents is not quite normal, and it should be remembered also that parents are almost always unsatisfactory to their children at this age."[1] Many books have been written to help parents understand their teen-agers and to help teen-agers understand themselves. In these few pages we highlight a few characteristics of this age. Books for further reading are suggested in the annotated book list in the back of this volume.

CONFLICT FOR THE TEEN-AGER

As was discussed in the previous chapter, early in the teen years a youngster begins a period of rapid physical growth and great physical change. Parents however, should see beyond the maturing body and the tremendous appetite and seek to understand something of the stress that goes on in the mind. This is a period of serious conflict within the teen-ager. He is in a transition from childhood to adulthood and wants to reach in both directions at the same time. He wants to be independent and yet is reluctant to give up his dependence.

Conflict exists, for instance, between his growing self-confidence and his sense of self-consciousness. He is aware of new power and possibilities, but often is still awkward and clumsy. Conflict exists between the powerful group consciousness or influence of the gang and his desire to be an individual and a nonconformist, between his desire for new experiences and his need for security. He finds his new experiences at school, with his group, or at times in daydreaming — where he dramatizes himself in some heroic situation. Yet the teen-ager needs the security of those who love and appreciate him. He manifests this desire for security by collecting things and seeking to achieve recognition or awards at school, in sports, and in community organizations.

Parents who are aware of these conflicts have at least some explanation of the inconsistent and erratic behavior of their teen-ager. They may never completely understand him, but they can stand by him with genuine concern and a love that tries to understand. This concern and love expresses itself by their interest in his affairs and activities, by their willingness to cooperate in his plans and listen to his ideas, by speaking words of praise and encouragement when they are able to, and by overlooking some of his irritating habits and faults.

PATIENCE FOR THE PARENT

"Where are you going tonight, Bob?" Mother innocently asked after the evening meal. "Out" was all he said. "What are you going to do?" she went on. "Nothing," was the answer this time. This is what to expect from a teen-ager. When he wants to share, he will talk. But not much is accomplished by nagging until he tells every detail of what he is going to do, nor by dictating to him what he should do. This is a time when the teen-ager needs to learn to make decisions for himself. It is a time for parents to be patient and let him make his own decisions on the basis of the groundwork that has been laid in previous years. This means trusting him and treating him as an intelligent human being.

The teen-ager wants parents who discuss with him the things he wants to discuss, thus helping him weigh the possibilities of a situation, and who then allow him to make the final decision. And he needs desperately to prove to himself and to his parents that he is capable of making that decision and keeping it. This is the way he matures, the way he tests and tries values and makes them his own.

It may be difficult for the teen-ager to come to his parents for help with his problems and decisions unless a warm and friendly relationship has been built and maintained from childhood. Often he finds it easier to talk to an adult counselor at school or church or in a community organization about his questions and doubts rather than his own parents. This should be expected and accepted.

During these years the young person is often making two of the most important decisions of his life: choosing a vocation and selecting a life partner. Parents cannot choose for him. They cannot dictate what their son will be or whom he will marry. In fact, the more they try, the more their son is likely to rebel and choose differently in an effort to express his independence. This is the nature of the teen-ager and young adult. In view of the necessity for personal choice and decision inherent in the nature of this age, parents must move into the background. This is how they can be of most help, guiding and correcting when necessary but always eager and ready to discuss and allow the teen-ager to make the final decision, respecting him as a maturing person with the right of personal choice.

It is in this approach that the young person is free to respond to the promptings of the Holy Spirit. The Spirit leads in many ways, through previous training and experience, through discussions, through searching the Scriptures, through prayer and meditation. Christian parents must be confident that even when a Christian young person makes a faulty choice, and everyone does, he still lives in God's forgiveness and is under God's control. As a matter of fact the assurance of God's forgiveness must be communicated through the parents' own forgiving attitude and through their helpful and understanding support.

TESTING FOR FAITH

Teen-age is a time of questions and doubts, a time of rethinking moral and ethical values. Robert Conrad describes a typical teen-age girl like this: "She has a hard time finding a satisfactory idea about God. . . . She feels depressed when she sees her failure to measure up to God's Law . . . at times she is not sure she is saved, even though she wants to find a deep faith in God. She wants God to have a deep personal meaning in her life, prayer to be a source of strength, and her Bible a rich help and 'comfort.' " [2]

One may tend to disagree with Professor Conrad's description of a Christian teen-ager when he notices the many dropouts from Bible class after confirmation and the lack of interest in attending church services during the teen years. There may be many reasons for this lack of church activity, but one of the important ones, Pastor Bueltmann[3] suggests in his booklet, is that the Bible class does not speak to the needs of the teen-ager, especially this questioning and searching spirit.

As the teen-ager moves toward adulthood, the boy's sexual drive reaches its highest peak. With it come the temptations of the parked car, the necking and petting, and at times the added can of beer or bottle of wine or whiskey. Often the teen-ager is caught in the middle and doesn't know how to control his desires. He is swept along with the gang, with what "everybody else is doing." This is a time of real testing. He needs to be prepared so he knows what to expect. He needs the constant sup-

94

port of devout Christian parents in a home that is conscious of the presence of God, where there is regular family devotion, where God is worshiped constantly and is served in deep love.

Courtship, Love, and Marriage

A 16-year-old girl complained that her parents had never told her anything about the things she wanted to know. Her mother, on the other hand, insisted that she had "told Anita everything." "But," said Anita, "I don't want to know only about sex, I want to know about being sexy." Actually, Dorothy Baruch said, "This is what is of greatest concern to both parents and youth." [4] How far should I go? How can I handle these feelings of anxiety about sex and self? This is the period when sex becomes very real and personal. The teen-ager no longer wonders how he was born or how people make babies, but "when can I have sexual relations?" "What will it be like for me to have a baby?" "How do I decide whom I will marry?"

This is the final crucial period in the sex guidance of children before they are adults. Parents must continue to build on what has been done in previous years. The relationship between child and parent is still very essential. If the teen-ager does not have the confidence to discuss his problems with his parents, if his parents do not trust him to make his own decisions on the basis of their training and suggestions, there really isn't much that can be done at this period. Scolding, complaining, forbidding will not help. Making strict rules will only encourage breaking them. Forbid the teen-ager to date a certain person and he may see her in secret; veto his planned marriage and he may elope.

If Christian parents know that this is the way young people often react, they will want to work with their adolescent and not against him. They will seek to discuss dating and how a Christian behaves on a date. They will show the advantages and the problems of a situation but leave the final decision to him. Some of the questions he will wonder about are these:

"Not really, although it seems like it at times. We each learn to love by being loved and by loving. This love experience starts when we are babies, and as a result of this being loved we learn to give and receive love. This is the foundation upon which our capacity for love as adults is built.

"Usually we come to love someone only after we know him and have been around him for a while. When you have a sudden feeling of attraction for someone it is often just an infatuation, one which might either die or grow into mature love. This kind of 'love at first sight' may be aroused by being close to someone or by sexual attraction. Sometimes we have a sudden feeling for someone because he is like another person we knew and respected and loved in our previous experience." [5]

"HOW CAN I BE SURE I AM IN LOVE?"

"There is no simple way of knowing whether your feeling for someone is an infatuation based on physical attraction and will soon pass away or whether it will become real love. Here are some things you can ask yourself as a personal check. But be honest!

"Are your thoughts centered more on the one you love than on yourself? Mature love seeks to make the object of that love happy and is not too concerned about the satisfaction and fun it gets for itself. It's something like the love of Jesus, who loved us enough to give His life for us. He was seeking to save us and not looking out for His own welfare.

"Do you respect and admire the one you love? Mature love cannot thrive unless there is a real liking for the kind of person you love and an admiration for the things he does.

"Will your love stand the test of time? This is the only real test that will tell how mature your love is. There is an old proverb which says, 'Never marry a man until you have summered and wintered with him.' More important than the seasons are the emotional climates that you weather together. 'If you have experienced together a wide gamut of emotions — sympathy, anger, resentment, sorrow, fear, hatred, as well as love — so that you know deep down inside how each of you feel under these conditions, then you can be said to know your loved one enough to expect the relationship to endure.' [6]

"As you search your heart with these questions pray that God lead you and be sure that you are willing to be led."

"WHAT ABOUT INTERFAITH MARRIAGE?"

"An interfaith marriage may be happy, but it has unique and fundamental problems. Marriage is a union of two people into 'one flesh,' physically, mentally, and spiritually. Disagreement on something as basic as one's religious beliefs and way of life can contribute little to the unity and happiness of marriage. In fact, it usually causes disagreements and problems. So if you are dating someone of another faith be careful about getting too serious. First talk over honestly your religious faith and attitudes. If you are strong in your faith, you will not want to give it up; and if he is strong in his, he will not want to give up his. And while you may respect each other, you will still live in disagreement. When children are born they will be torn by divided loyalties. It is better to part as friends, for marriage has enough problems without adding difficulty by mixing religion. Of course, if your partner is ready to accept your faith and is willing to join your church that is another thing. But by all means settle it before you decide to marry." [7]

"SHOULD YOU GET MARRIED IF YOU ARE PREGNANT?"

"If you had planned to marry before you became pregnant, then getting married may be a good solution to the problem you have made for yourself. But you ought to go to a counselor first and talk it over before you do anything: your minister, a marriage counselor, or a social worker at a family agency. If you are emotionally ready for marriage and are suited to each other, marriage is fine. But if you had not been discussing marriage, or if it looks as if your marriage would be difficult and full of problems, then marriage may be the wrong solution. Two wrongs don't make a right. It may be best to let a child welfare agency arrange to place the baby for adoption. You can go to a special home for unwed mothers and have it arranged without too much difficulty.

"One of the serious problems a girl has to face if she becomes pregnant outside of marriage is spiritual. She usually feels guilt for having sinned against her Lord and ashamed for having brought disgrace to her family. She needs a lot of love and understanding from her parents and the assurance that they are ready to forgive and help her. She needs at this time a full understanding of what forgiveness of sins means as applied to her situation. And she needs, besides, loyal friends, relatives, and deep spiritual resources to help her face her dilemma."

"WHY SHOULDN'T TEEN-AGERS GET MARRIED?"

"Usually because they are not ready for it. Some teen-agers do get married and make a go of it, but the chances for a successful and happy marriage are much less than for those who marry later. One study showed that 60 percent of the marriages in which bride and groom were between 18 and 21 ended in divorce. But when the age was 25 or older, only 30 percent ended in divorce. The same study showed that 40 percent of those who marry as teen-agers do so because the girl is pregnant.[8]

"To make a happy and successful marriage one must learn from experience how to handle his emotions, how to get along with others, how to adjust to others, and how to give and take. We learn these things during our teens as we date and court, work and play. When we shorten the time for these learning experiences and hurry into marriage, we cheat ourselves of this maturing process. Usually the marriage suffers."

Sexual Intercourse

"You mean your dad talked to you about how a fellow gets all excited when he necks with a girl?" Fred asked his friend

Jim. "Sure," Jim answered, "we've always had talks, and we cover any subject I want."

Fred was almost envious. "I couldn't talk to my dad like that. If I ever brought up the subject, he'd probably blow his stack and tell me to stay away from girls."

Most teen-agers, sad to say, are like Fred. They can't talk to their fathers or mothers about such intimate subjects, although deep within they have many questions about which they would like to talk. One of the things that fills the growing adolescent with wonder is the sex act itself. In answering questions, parents ought to keep sexual relations in the framework of their natural purpose in God's creation. Intercourse is a way of expressing love and surrender in becoming "one flesh" in marriage. It is an enjoyable experience. It is God's way of creating new life. Some questions which usually come to the adolescent are these:

"WHAT'S WRONG WITH SEXUAL RELATIONS BEFORE MARRIAGE?"

"I'm sure you understand that God made intercourse for marriage. It is such an intimate act that it cannot really fulfill its unique function according to God's plan outside of marriage — certainly not in a parked car! The sex act is supposed to be the climax of a love relationship between two people who have married and live together and share life together. It is an expression of the deep, lasting, personal relationship that exists between husband and wife. It expresses the total unity that they share as husband and wife. Before marriage there is no such unity to express and physical intimacies become merely a satisfaction of physical desires. True love is always more than that. Be sure not to think of love and sex as synonymous."

"DO ALL MARRIED COUPLES HAVE INTERCOURSE?"

"Normally, yes. Marriage without sexual union is regarded as not consummated and therefore no marriage. Intercourse is a privilege and duty of marriage. The union of man and woman is so complete that the Bible speaks of husband and wife as being 'one flesh.' St. Paul even says that spouses normally have no right to refuse intercourse to each other except by agreement for a certain period of time and then for an adequate reason (1 Cor. 7:2-5). Couples must agree between themselves when and how often they will have sexual relations. Some desire them every day, some several times a week, some once a week or only once a month."

"AREN'T YOU AFRAID THE FIRST TIME YOU HAVE INTERCOURSE?"

"Many brides are afraid that it will hurt, and often the young bridegroom is nervous because he is not sure just how to act. But if you really love each other and let yourself make love and be loved, sexual relations will soon seem natural and right. Skill develops as each learns to know and understand the other better. There are good books to help you prepare for this experience, and you will want to read one before you get married." [9]

"DO ALL PEOPLE ENJOY SEXUAL RELATIONS?"

"Men are more easily aroused sexually than women, and so they almost always enjoy sexual relations. Many women enjoy them just as much, and this is the way it should be. Yet there are some women who do not enjoy intercourse as completely as others, usually because of fear and tension. Even so, a Christian wife will take part in intercourse as a duty of marriage to satisfy her husband. She may gradually come to enjoy it as she overcomes her tensions and is able to surrender more completely. The deepest satisfaction comes not from the fulfillment of biological urges but from the fulfillment of the relationship of two people. A man or woman who cannot enjoy sexual relations is called 'frigid.' This often results from the training of feelings about sex in childhood. Frigidity is much more frequent in women than in men. A husband whose wife has difficulty enjoying sexual relations needs to give a lot of love, patience, and understanding in order to help her as much as possible. If all else fails, it would be well to see a doctor for a physical examination and perhaps a psychiatrist to discuss the causes of frigidity."

Having Babies

"WHY CAN'T SOME COUPLES HAVE CHILDREN?"

"Sometimes a married couple does not have children because either the husband or wife is sterile. A woman is sterile when for some reason the regular monthly ovum is not released or placed in a position where it can be fertilized. A man is sterile when he is not able to produce sperm that can fertilize the ovum. If the cause of sterility is a physical disorder, it may be corrected by a doctor. Sometimes it is caused by an emotional block and might be discussed with a counselor or psychiatrist."

"WHAT IS BIRTH CONTROL (PLANNED PARENTHOOD)?"

"Birth control is preventing the conception of a baby. This is done by different methods using what are called 'contraceptives.' One of the most popular methods is the use of a condom, a rubber sheath or sack placed over the penis to prevent the semen from entering the vagina. Sometimes a woman will be fitted with a diaphragm which covers the cervix or opening to the uterus. This diaphragm used with a jelly prevents the male sperm from getting to the egg. Another way is to use jelly, cream, foam, or some other chemical preparation to destroy the sperm and prevent the sperm from fertilizing the egg. The latest method is to take a pill orally which prevents the woman's ovaries from releasing the egg into her tube." (More details are given in the Appendix on "Methods of Contraception.")

"These methods of birth control are often used to plan a family or space children. The Christian wants to fulfill that part of the purpose of sex and marriage which involves having children, receiving them as gifts from God, and training them for Him. Complete prevention of conception, unless for good reasons, thwarts one of the basic purposes of marriage. Good reasons for the Christian to use birth control include especially the health of the mother, and spacing or planning the family. The latter is called "planned parenthood."

101

"WHAT IS A MISCARRIAGE?"

"When a baby is born before it has developed enough to live outside of the mother's body, we call this a miscarrage. This expelling of the undeveloped baby happens if there is something wrong in the development of the fertilized cell or if there is some weakness in the mother's body which prevents the baby from staying alive and growing in her uterus. Miscarriage may also be caused by illness or by injury to the mother. Normally a baby cannot live outside of the mother's body before it is 6½ to 7 months old."

"WHAT IS A CAESAREAN BIRTH?"

"If the baby cannot be born through the vagina because there is something physically wrong, the doctor will perform an operation and remove the baby through an opening he makes in the mother's abdomen. This is called a Caesarean birth because Julius Caesar decreed that if a mother died, the infant could be delivered this way. This does not hurt the baby if it is mature enough, and it does not harm the mother, although she will have to be inactive longer so that the incision can heal properly."

"WHAT IS IT LIKE TO BE IN LABOR?"

"Most women are a little nervous and have some misgivings about the birth of the first baby because they have heard so much about the 'labor' or 'contractions.' The contractions feel like sharp stomach cramps which go all the way through to the back. They are caused by the stretching and contracting of muscles. First the fibrous tissue of the cervix, the opening of the uterus into the vagina, must stretch in order to let the baby pass through into the vagina. The vagina too must stretch large enough to let the baby pass out into the outside world. Sometime during the process the membrane which holds the fluid in which the baby floats breaks. (Sometimes people refer to this as 'rupture of the bag of water.')"

The Homosexual

"WHAT IS A HOMOSEXUAL?"

"A homosexual is a person who focuses too much love upon himself. His emotions have not matured enough for him to be able to give love to people of the other sex. He prefers instead someone of the same sex to satisfy his emotional and sexual desires. Sometimes this is but a temporary step in the process by which emotions mature; sometimes, however, it becomes a deep-seated problem which makes this person a poor marriage risk. More men become homosexual than women. In women it is often called lesbianism."

"CAN A HOMOSEXUAL BE CURED?"

"If a person has been a homosexual for some time, he is very difficult to cure. Some, who really want to change, can be cured with the help of a psychiatrist. The Christian understands that this way of sexual satisfaction is contrary to the normal, God-given use for sex. A Christian who gets caught in this web and develops homosexual tendencies has a hard struggle to face. He needs a full measure of the Savior's grace. It may help him to remember that his body is a creation of God, which has been redeemed and become the temple of the Holy Spirit."

"HOW CAN I TELL WHO IS A HOMOSEXUAL?"

"The only way you can tell who is a homosexual is from the advances he makes toward you. He tries to get very friendly and may start by wanting to touch and feel you, which is the beginning of wanting you to take part in his abnormal sex acts. If that ever happens, refuse to let him touch you and leave."

"HOW CAN I TELL WHETHER I HAVE HOMOSEXUAL TENDENCIES?"

"It is easy to exaggerate one's feelings and expand them into whatever lies upon one's mind. Be careful about doing that with sexual feelings. Perhaps the most important signal to look for in determining whether one has homosexual tendencies is contact with those of your own sex. Do you want to touch them and kiss them? Do you enjoy being with one person of the same sex and love this person in a possessive way? If you suspect that you have homosexual tendencies, talk to someone who can help you, such as your doctor or your pastor."

General Questions

"WHAT IS A PROSTITUTE (HARLOT)?"

"A prostitute or harlot is a woman who participates in sexual relations for pay. She allows men to use her body for money. There are also male prostitutes, who let women or homosexual men use their bodies as they please to satisfy their desires. A prostitute is misusing the body and the gift of sex which God has given, making of sex a 'thing,' a commodity for sale, rather than an expression of love. The Bible speaks strongly in condemning prostitution."

"HOW CAN YOU TELL IF YOU HAVE V. D.?"

"The main venereal diseases, that is, diseases spread by sexual intercourse, are gonorrhea and syphilis. Gonorrhea (gon-or-REE-a) is an infection of the sex organ and urinary tract and causes a burning pain when a person urinates (but not every burning sensation is a sign of gonorrhea). Syphilis (SIF-ill-is) is a general infection in the bloodstream which shows up first with an open sore in the genital area and then spreads through the bloodstream. These first sores may disappear for a while, even if you don't do anything about them, but the infection is still there spreading through the bloodstream. Modern drugs are able to cure both of these diseases in their early stages. To be sure that the person you marry does not have V. D., blood tests are required in most states."

"WHAT DOES IT MEAN TO BE STERILE?"

"A sterile person is one who is not fertile, who does not have the power to reproduce. This may be the result of some deformity in the reproductive organs or it may be a result of surgery, an operation called 'sterilization.' In the woman the Fallopian tubes are severed by a surgeon, so that no ovum and sperm may join. In the man a similar operation severs the vas deferens, the duct which carries the sperm from the testes to the urethra of the penis. Laws regulating sterilization have been adopted by most states and some of the provinces of Canada to regulate the sterilization operation.

"Christians have serious questions about too free a use of sterilization because it is taking away from a man or woman the power to reproduce what is a blessing of God and intended to be a part of marriage."

"WHAT DO I TELL KIDS WHO WANT ME TO JOIN A NONVIRGIN CLUB?"

"I know you want to be accepted by the other kids at school, but it's not worth it if you have to sacrifice your virtue and live with a guilty conscience. You just have to face up to it. Sexual relations belong in marriage. Tell them you will not have intercourse before marriage because you love your Savior Jesus. He died for you, and you are going to live for Him. You will find others who feel like this at your church, and there you can have a crowd of Christians to chum with."

FOOTNOTES FOR CHAPTER VII

1. Audrey J. Williamson, *Your Teen-Ager and You* (Anderson, Ind.: The Warner Press, n. d.), p. 12.
2. Robert L. Conrad, "Reaching for Adulthood," *The Growing Child,* Parent Guidance Series No. 11 (St. Louis: Concordia Publishing House, 1962), p. 49.

3. August J. Bueltmann, *Teen-Agers Need Parents,* Parent Guidance Series No. 4 (St. Louis: Concordia Publishing House, n. d.)

4. Dorothy Walter Baruch, *New Ways in Sex Education* (New York: McGraw-Hill Book Company, Inc., 1959), p. 207.

5. For some good chapters on love read Evelyn Millis Duvall, *Love and the Facts of Life* (New York: Association Press, 1963), pp. 14—75.

6. Ibid.

7. See a book like James Pike, *If You Marry Outside Your Faith* (New York: Harper & Brothers, 1954).

8. Lloyd Shearer, "Date Early! Marry Late!" *Parade* (May 13, 1962). pp. 6—7.

9. A standard book used often in premarital counseling is S. A. Lewis and John Gilmore, *Sex Without Fear* (New York: Medical Research Press, 1950).

VIII.
Glossary
Of Terms

Abdomen (AB-domen)
The lower part of the trunk of the body, commonly referred to as the stomach or belly.

Abortion (a-BOR-shun)
Expulsion of unborn child before viability. Performing an abortion is illegal, unless there is a medical indication for doing it.

Abstinence (AB-stin-ence)
Voluntarily abstaining. In marriage it refers to refraining from sexual intercourse.

Acne (AK-nee)
The condition of an adolescent's complexion characterized by pimples and blackheads.

Adrenal (ad-RE-nal)
The little glands which sit like cocked hats on top of the kidneys. They make substances (hormones) that control the body metabolism.

Adultery (a-DULL-ter-ee)
Intercourse with a person who is already married to someone else. Sometimes used to refer to any intercourse outside of marriage.

Afterbirth
The placenta which is expelled after the birth of a baby.

Amnion (AM-nee-on)
One of the membranes which form the double sac of water in which the baby floats in the uterus to protect it.

Anus (A-nus)
The opening at the base of the buttocks which is the passage by which waste material is discharged from the intestines.

Areola (a-REE-o-la)

The dark area around the nipple of the female breast.

Axillary (AK-si-la-ree) *hair*

Hair which grows under the arms.

Bastard (BAS-tard)

A child born out of wedlock, also known as an illegitimate child.

Bladder (BLAD-er)

A sac in the pelvic region for the temporary storage of urine.

Caesarean (si-SAR-ee-an) *section*

The delivery of a child through an incision in the abdomen made by a surgeon when for some reason the mother cannot have a normal birth.

Cervix (SER-vix)

The neck of the womb, part of which extends into the vagina.

Chancre (SHANG-ker)

A little sore, usually on the genitals, which is the first symptom of syphilis.

Chorion (KOR-ee-on)

One of the membranes which form the double sac filled with water in which the baby floats in the mother's uterus.

Circumcision (ser-kum-SIZH-un)

The minor operation of cutting away the loose skin (foreskin) from the end of the penis. Circumcision is a rite used by the Jews, the ceremony of reception into their faith. Today many people circumcise for the purposes of cleanliness.

Climacteric (cly-MACK-teric)

The change of life for the male, usually occurring between the ages of 50 and 60. Men may be subject to feelings of failure vocationally, economically, or spiritually at this time.

Climax (KLY-max)

The highest point of excitement in sexual intercourse, often called the orgasm.

Clitoris (KLIT-or-is)

A small, sensitive female sex organ located where the inner folds of the vulva meet, similar to a tiny penis.

Cohabitation (co-hab-i-TAY-shun)

Sexual intercourse.

Coitus (CO-i-tus)

The sex act.

Conception (kon-SEP-shun)

The beginnings of the organism which will grow into a baby. This happens when the sperm enters the female egg.

Concubine (CON-cue-bine)

A woman who lives with a man as his wife, even though they are not married.

Condom (CON-dum)

A rubber sheath placed over the penis during intercourse to prevent the semen from entering the vagina.

Congenital (con-GEN-i-tal)

Existing from birth. A congenital deformity is one with which a child is born.

Conjugal (CON-ju-gal)

Pertaining to marriage, as conjugal love.

Contraception (con-tra-SEP-shun)

The prevention of conception by preventing the sperm and the egg from meeting or by destroying their ability to fertilize.

Copulation (cop-yoo-LAY-shun)

Sexual intercourse.

Cowper's (COO-pers) *gland*

Two small glands near the base of the bladder which discharge secretions into the male urethra to lubricate it prior to ejection of semen.

Defecate (DEF-e-cate)

To discharge waste material from the intestine through the anus.

Depilatories (dee-PILL-a-tor-eez)

Hair removers.

Diaphragm (DIE-a-fram)

A thin rubber disk placed over the entrance to the womb to prevent the male sperm, during intercourse, from entering and fertilizing the female egg.

Douche (DOOSH)

The washing of the vagina by a stream of water injected with a syringe. Also a device for giving douches.

Ejaculate (ee-JACK-yoo-late)

To discharge semen from the penis.

Embryo (EM-bree-oh)

An animal in the earliest stages of its beginning. In humans it refers to the fertilized seed during the first 8 weeks of its growth in the mother's womb.

Endometrium (en-do-MEE-tree-um)

The glandular lining of the uterus which thickens and fills with blood and nutrients when a ripe ovum is expected.

Enzyme (EN-zime)

A chemical substance produced by cells. The sperm produces a special kind of enzyme to help it pierce the outer membrane of the eggshell.

Epididymis (ep-i-DID-i-mis)

A tube made up of a mass of coils in back of each testicle, where the sperm are stored temporarily until they travel up into the body.

Erection (ee-RECK-shun)

The hardening and stiffening of the penis as the blood fills the spongy tissue during sexual excitement.

Eunuch (YOO-nuck)

A man who has had his testicles removed. He is not able to produce sperm or the male hormone.

Exhibitionist (eck-si-BISH-un-ist)

When referring to the sexual use, one who exposes his genitals to attract the attention of others.

Fallopian (fa-LO-pee-an) *tubes*

The tubes into and through which the egg released by the ovary travels to the uterus.

Feces (FEE-sez)

The waste matter passed out of the body through the anus, sometimes called "stool."

Fecundate (FEE-kun-date)

The male sperm joining the female egg to begin the growth of a baby.

Fertilize (FUR-til-ize)

The male sperm joining the female egg to begin the growth of a baby.

Fetus (FEE-tus)

A baby in the mother's womb after the first 8 weeks. Before this it is called an "embryo."

Fontanels (font-en-ELS)

The spaces between the five large bony plates which make up the skull of a baby. When the baby is born, these spaces allow the baby's head bones to squeeze together so it can pass through the cervix and vagina. One of them is called the "soft spot" on the top of the baby's head.

Foreplay

The petting and caressing which stimulates sexual desires before intercourse.

Foreskin

The loose skin which covers the end of the penis. It is removed in circumcision.

Frigidity (fri-JID-ity)

The inability of a person to respond to sexual stimulation.

Gland

An organ of the body. Some glands are used for the elimination of waste, like the sweat gland. Other glands produce a substance which affects growth and development, such as the pituitary, thyroid, adrenal, ovaries, and testes. Still others aid digestion, such as the pancreatic glands.

Glans penis

The rounded head of the penis which is exposed after circumcision or when the foreskin is pushed back.

Gonads (GO-nads)

The sex glands, ovaries in women and testicles in men.

Gonococcus (gon-o-COCK-us)

A bacteria which causes gonorrhea.

Gonorrhea (gon-or-REE-a)

A disease of the inside lining of the male or female sex organs, characterized by burning, painful urination and a discharge.

Gynecologist (gin-e-COLL-o-gist)

A doctor who specializes in the treament of the diseases of women.

Harlot

A woman who allows men to have intercourse with her for pay.

Hermaphroditism (hur-MAF-ro-dite-ism)

Being born with both male and female sex organs.

Homosexual (hoh-mo-SESK-shoo-al)

A person who wants to satisfy his sex desires with a person of the same sex. Some popular synonyms for homosexual are fairy, queer, fruit, queen, fag. A female homosexual is often called a lesbian.

Hormone (HOR-mown)

A chemical substance which is formed in a gland of the body and is carried by the blood to other parts of the body, where it stimulates some special activity.

111

Hymen (HIGH-men)

A rim of soft tissue which partially closes the entrance to the vagina.

Hysterectomy (hys-ter-ECK-toe-mee)

The operation in which the complete uterus is removed.

Illegitimate (ill-le-JIT-a-mit) *child*

A child whose mother and father have not married by the time he is born. Also known as a bastard.

Impotence (IM-poe-tence)

Lack of the ability of the man to achieve the erection necessary for intercourse.

Incest (IN-sest)

Sexual intercourse between blood relatives.

Intercourse (IN-ter-course)

The sex act, in which the husband places his penis in the vagina of the wife and ejects his semen.

Kahn test

A test of the blood to determine the presence of syphilis.

Labor

The work of the muscles of the uterus as they push the baby out of the mother's body in birth.

Lesbianism (LES-bee-an-ism)

A form of sexual perversion where one woman receives satisfaction from another woman. Other terms used are tribadism and sapphism. The name comes from the Aegean island of Lesbos, where in ancient times female homosexuality was sometimes practiced as a part of religious rites.

Masochism (MASS-o-kism)

A form of sexual perversion in which a person receives pleasure from being dominated by another or from being beaten, humiliated, or harshly handled in other ways.

Masturbation (mas-tur-BAY-shun)

Satisfying sexual desires by manipulating one's own sex organs, often to the point of climax.

Menarche (me-NAR-key)

The beginning of menstruation in a woman.

Menopause (MEN-o-pause)

The change of life in a woman when she stops menstruating, usually between 45 and 50.

Menses (MEN-seez)

The flow of blood from the vagina as the uterus sheds the lining it prepared for the growth of a baby.

Menstruation (men-stroo-AY-shun)

The discharge through the vagina of the cells which lined the womb in preparation for growth of a baby. This "period" occurs about every 28–30 days.

Miscarriage (mis-CARE-ij)

The birth of a baby before it is mature enough to live.

Misogynist (miss-OJ-i-nist)

A man who is afraid of marriage or who hates women.

Narcissism (NAR-cis-sism)

Extreme love of oneself.

Navel (NAY-vel)

The mark or depression in the abdomen where the umbilical cord was attached.

Nocturnal emissions (seminal emissions or wet dreams)

The passing of semen from the male during sleep, experienced by most adolescent boys as a normal function of their sex organs.

Nymphomaniac (nim-foe-MAY-nee-ack)

A woman who suffers from excessive sexual desire.

Obstetrician (ob-ste-TRISH-un)

A physician who treats women during pregnancy and childbirth.

Orgasm (OR-gasm)

The climax of sexual intercourse, accompanied by high excitement. In men this is accompanied by the ejection of semen.

Ovary (OH-va-ree)

Two almond-shaped glands which are the sex glands of a woman. They produce the tiny eggs or ova which are the female reproductive cells. The ovaries also produce a hormone which causes the female characteristics of rounding of the hips and development of the breasts.

Ovulation (oh-vyoo-LAY-shun)

The discharge of the ripe egg from the ovary to the Fallopian tube, which occurs every 26–30 days.

Ovum (OH-vum)

The female reproductive cell (egg) found in the ovary. The plural is "ova."

Pancreas (PANG-cre-us)

A gland near the stomach which makes a substance that mixes with food to aid digestion. It also makes insulin to prevent diabetes.

Penis (PEE-niss)

The male sex organ through which urine is passed and semen is discharged.

Pituitary (pi-TYOO-i-ter-ee)

A gland inside the skull at the base of the brain which is in charge of all the other ductless glands.

Placenta (pla-SEN-ta)

The organ of spongy blood cells by which the baby is attached to the lining of the uterus. It serves to feed the baby and to dispose of waste. The umbilical cord connects the placenta and the baby.

Pregnant (PREG-nant)

The condition of a woman from the time a baby begins to grow in her body until it is born.

Prenatal (pre-NAY-tal)

Before birth.

Prepuce (PREE-pyoos)

The loose skin that covers the end of the penis, which is removed in circumcision. Sometimes it is called the "foreskin."

Prostitute (PROSS-ti-tute)

A woman who allows men to have intercourse with her for pay. A male prostitute sells the use of his body to male homosexuals or to women.

Prostate (PROSS-tate) *gland*

A gland at the base of the bladder which secretes a fluid that becomes part of the semen. Middle-aged men often have trouble when this gland grows too large and prevents proper urination.

Puberty (PEW-bur-tee)

The period of rapid physical development that marks the end of childhood and the beginning of maturation. Sex organs mature and produce sex cells.

Pubic (PEW-bic)

Concerning the lower part of the abdomen, where hair grows in a triangular patch.

Rape

The act of forcing a woman to have intercourse without her consent.

Rectum (RECK-tum)
The lower end of the large intestine, which extends to the anus.

Sadism (SAD-ism)
A form of sexual perversion in which a person receives satisfaction from inflicting pain on another or seeing another person suffer pain.

Sanitary napkins
Pads used by women during menstruation to absorb the menstrual flow.

Sapphism (SAF-ism)
A form of sexual perversion where one woman receives satisfaction from another woman. Also called lesbianism and tribadism. The name comes from the Greek woman poet Sappho, who practiced homosexuality on the island of Lesbos.

Scrotum (SKROH-tum)
The sack of skin, suspended between the male's legs, which contains the testicles.

Semen (SEE-men)
The male sperm cells together with a whitish fluid that is discharged through the penis.

Seminal emissions (SEM-i-nal ee-MISH-uns)
The passing of semen from the male during sleep, experienced by most normal adolescent boys. Often it is accompanied by dreams.

Seminal vesicle (SEM-i-nal VESS-i-cal)
A storage sac for male sperm cells after they are produced in the testicles.

Smegma (SMEG-ma)
A secretion of the sex organ. In the male it accumulates under the foreskin of the penis and needs to be washed away regularly.

Soft spot
See fontanel.

Sperm, spermatozoa (sper-ma-to-ZOE-a)
The male cells which fertilize the female egg. Shaped like a tadpole with a head and an active tail, they are made in the testes. They enter the female egg in fertilization.

Spermatic cord (same as vas deferens)
The tube through which the sperm is brought from the epididymis to the seminal vesicles.

115

Spirochetes (SPY-roe-keets)

Little corkscrewlike germs which cause syphilis. They burrow into body tissue and often lie dormant for years.

Sterilization (ster-ill-i-ZAY-shun)

A process wherein a man or woman is made sterile, that is, unable to produce children. They can still have intercourse.

Syphilis (SIF-ill-is)

A venereal disease which first appears as a small painless ulcer in the genital area and spreads through the bloodstream to the entire body.

Tampon (TAM-pon)

A soft tight roll of absorbent material which can be inserted into the vagina to soak up the menstrual flow. Used instead of sanitary napkins or menstrual pads.

Testes (TES-teez) (testicles)

Male sex glands in a sac between the legs. These glands produce the male sperm and a hormone which causes the male characteristics of voice change, hair growth, etc.

Testosterone (test-TOSS-ter-own)

The hormone, secreted by the testicles into the blood, which helps the development of a boy into a man.

Testicle (TESS-ti-kal)

One of the two male sex organs suspended between the legs in a sac. These organs produce the male sperm and a hormone which causes the male characteristics of voice change, hair growth, etc.

Thyroid (THY-roid)

A gland in the neck which is responsible for some of our mental and physical growth.

Tribadism (TRIB-ad-ism)

A form of sexual perversion in which one woman receives satisfaction from another woman. Also called lesbianism and sapphism.

Umbilical (um-BILL-i-cal) *cord*

The cord which connects the baby to the tissue in the womb and through which it is fed.

Ureter (yoo-REE-ter)

Duct by which the urine passes from the kidney to the bladder.

Urethra (Yoo-REE-thra)

The duct through which the urine passes out of the body from the bladder. In males it also carries the discharge of semen.

Uterus (YOO-ter-us)

A muscular organ of the female reproductive system shaped like a pear with the larger end up. Here is where the fertilized egg grows into a baby. The normal uterus holds a teaspoon of liquid, but when a baby grows inside it stretches like a balloon.

Urine (YOO-rin)

A pale yellow fluid manufactured by the kidneys from waste in the blood, stored in the bladder, and passed out of the body as waste through the urethra.

Vagina (va-JY-na)

The passageway which connects the uterus or womb with the outside of the body, between the legs of the woman

Vas deferens (vas DEF-er-enz)

The tube through which the sperm are carried from the testicles into the penis.

Venereal (ve-NEE-ree-al) *disease*

A disease, such as gonorrhea and syphilis, which is spread mainly through sex relations.

Virgin (VER-jin)

A woman who has never had sexual relations with a man, or a man who has never had sexual relations with a woman.

Vulva (VUL-va)

Folds of skin and flesh which protect the opening of the vagina between the legs of a woman.

Wasserman test

A test of the blood to determine present or past infection with the syphilitic organism.

Annotated Book List

Cockefair, Edgar, and Ada Milam. *The Story of You.* Madison Wis.: Monona Publications, 1955.

> A picture book to be read to small children. It uses children's drawings to explain how the egg grows into a "fuzzy ball" — and then a baby in the "sack" called the uterus, like in a "cozy little nest."

Ets, Marie Hall. *The Story of a Baby.* New York: The Viking Press, 1939.

> This is one of the first books printed for small children on this subject. In 63 large pages, drawings and read-aloud story tell the development of a baby in its "house" from a speck too small to see to its birth.

Frey, Marguerite Kurth. *I Wonder, I Wonder.* St. Louis: Concordia Publishing House, 1967. 30 pp. $1.75. K—grade 3.

Selsam, Millicent. *All About Eggs and How They Change into Animals.* New York: William R. Scott, Inc., 1952.

> An attractive picture book which shows how fish and birds and animals come out of eggs. With drawings it shows how some eggs with the babies in them grow inside of their mothers. The ending shows that "you too grew inside of your mother."

Shane, Ruth and Harold. *The New Baby.* New York: Golden Press, 1957.

> A little Golden Book describing how Mike was prepared for the coming of a baby sister.

Appell, Clara, and Morey and Suzanne Szass. *We Are Six.* New York: Golden Press, 1959.

> This is a picture book which uses one to three actual photographs on each page with only a few lines of text. It tells the warm story of a family living together and welcoming a new baby, making a total of six.

Gruenberg, Sidonie Matsner. *The Wonderful Story of How You Were Born.* Garden City, New York: Doubleday and Co., 1952.

Prepared like a small child's picture book, it can be used in a number of ways. At 4 the child can look at the pictures as you tell the story. At 6 or 7 it can be read to the child. When the child is able to read, he can read it for himself. Pictures are of a general nature.

Hummel, Ruth Stevenson. *Wonderfully Made.* St. Louis: Concordia Publishing House, 1967. 46 pp. $1.75. Grades 4—6.

Levine, Milton I., and Jean H. Seligmann. *A Baby Is Born: the Story of How Life Begins.* New York: Golden Press, 1962.

With simple drawings and easy-reading text, this book shows and tells how life begins when the sperm and the egg join in the uterus. The sex organs, intercourse, growth, and birth are all covered. Very well done, but without God.

Warner, Hugh C. *Where Did I Come From?* St. Louis: Concordia Publishing House, 1963.

A booklet which can be read to children. It explains in a beautiful, Christian way where I came from, using several pictures. Only 10 small pages.

Whiting, Ellis W. *The Story of Life.* Milwaukee: Hammond Publishing Co., 1957.

A small, plastic, spiral-bound book, in which a father tells a story of how a baby is made and born. It can be read to children about 6 and older. He starts with a comparison with a flower and its "sex organs." Some answers to specific questions are listed in the back. Good though brief.

CHILDREN 8—13

Bueltmann, August J. *Take the High Road.* St. Louis: Concordia Publishing House, 1967. 88 pp. $1.95. Grades 7—9.

Butterfield, Frances Westgate. *From Little Acorns: The Story of Your Body.* New York: Renbayle House Publishers, Inc., 1951.

The interesting story of how David and Judy Jones learn about the growth and development of the human body. One chapter deals with "Male and Female" and how babies are born. Uses line drawings to explain the birth of a baby.

Clarkson, E. Margaret. *Chats with Young People on Growing Up.* Grand Rapids: Wm. B. Eerdmans Publishing Company, 1962.

A sequel to *Susie's Babies.*

Clarkson, E. Margaret. *Susie's Babies.* Grand Rapids: Wm. B. Eerdmans Publishing Company, 1960.

The true story of how 35 children and their teacher talk frankly and honestly about mating, conception, birth and rearing of children, using as their starting point Susie and Lue, a pair of pet hamsters and their eight babies. Drawings are only of hamsters and not humans.

The Gift of Life. New York: Mental Health Materials Center, n. d.

This 25-cent picture book shows changes that occur in boys' and girls' bodies from 9 to 12. Very helpful for parents and can be used with young people in the home.

Lerrigo, Marion O., and Helen Southard. *Finding Yourself*. Chicago: American Medical Association, 1961.

The book in the series of five intended for the junior-high level child to read as he or she begins dating and notices the development of the sex organs. Uses line drawings to explain sex and birth.

———. *A Story About You*. Chicago: American Medical Association, 1964.

One in the series of five books for different age levels. The children in grades 4—6 can read this and look at the line drawings of human growth and sex anatomy of boys and girls. Very frank but well done.

Lerrigo, Marion O., and Michael A. Cassidy. *A Doctor Talks to 9—12 Year Olds*. Chicago: Budlong Press Co., 1964.

An excellent booklet distributed by doctors which explains the story of life to children of this age, in readable language and simple line drawings. It is especially concerned with the changes in boys and girls of this age both in their physical makeup and in their feelings. The companion booklet, *Your Child from 9—12*, is given to parents at the same time.

Warner Sex Education Series: Hugh C. Warner. *How the Family Begins* (girls). *The Start of a Family* (boys).

These are good booklets to have boys and girls from about 10 to 15 read for themselves, for they tell the story in a warm, Christian way. The pages are small, and there are only 13 of them.

TEEN-AGERS

Behlmer, Reuben. *From Teens to Marriage*. St. Louis: Concordia Publishing House, 1959.

Discusses the physical and psychological problems of teen-agers and young adults. No pictures or drawings. Good sections on courtship and marriage.

Duvall, Evelyn Millis. *Love and the Facts of Life*. New York: Association Press, 1963.

Recognized as one of the best books on helping teen-agers understand sex and love. Good sections on dating and petting.

Duvall, Evelyn Millis, *Why Wait Till Marriage*. New York: Association Press, 1965. Paperback 1968.

Brings to bear on the problem of how far love-making should go, before marriage, all the relevant findings in the areas of social and medical science as well as religion.

Lerrigo, Marion O., and Helen Southard. *Approaching Adulthood*. Chicago: American Medical Association, n. d.

One of a five-booklet series, intended for ages 16—20. It reviews the basic facts of sex and helps young people in their choice of a marriage partner, suggesting ways to make marriage work.

Mozes, Eugene B. *Sex Facts and Fiction for Teen-Agers.* New York: Medical Research Press, 1957.

A doctor discusses in a simple, factual way the age of the adolescent and the problems he faces in growing up, especially in the area of sex. The author covers all the facts from prostitution to homosexuals. There are only five sketchy line drawings to illustrate sex and birth.

Riess, Walter. *For You, Teen-Ager in Love.* St. Louis: Concordia Publishing House, 1960.

Written from a fine Christian point of view, this little book seeks to help teen-agers meet the temptations of courtship and find the right marriage partner.

Sakol, Jeanne. *What About Teen-Age Marriage?* New York: Julian Messner, Inc., 1961.

A book for teen-age girls and parents to help them think through the things involved in teen-age marriage.

Shedd, Charlie W., *The Stork Is Dead.* Waco, Texas: Word Books, 1968.

After years of answering teen-agers' letters about sex in *Teen* magazine in Hollywood, the author shares some of his experiences in "telling teen-agers how it is." The same author wrote his advice for marriage in *Letters to Karen* and *Letters to Phillip.*

Soehren, Irene. *Why Love Asks You to Wait.* St. Louis: Concordia Publishing House, 1964.

A 23-page pamphlet which summons positive and negative reasons to convince the teen-ager to reserve intercourse for marriage.

Witt, Elmer. *Life Can Be Sexual.* St. Louis: Concordia Publishing House, 1967. $1.95

PARENTS

Amstutz, H. Clair. *Growing Up to Love: A Guide to Sex Education for Parents.* Scottdale, Pa.: Herald Press, 1956.

A doctor writes this book to encourage parents to provide sex information not merely at the right time but connected with the deeper meanings of life in the context of love in the family.

Baruch, Dorothy Walter. *New Ways in Sex Education.* New York: McGraw-Hill Book Co., Inc., 1959.

A professor and psychologist offers a guide to parents and teachers in making sex education a part of the complete development of the child. Very complete, including illustrative and true experiences, but without religious view.

Bracher, Marjory Louise. *Love Is No Luxury.* Philadelphia, Pa.: Fortress Press, 1951; rev. ed. 1961.

A good help to understanding the problems of learning to live as a family, with Christian suggestions to serve as a guide.

Bro, Marguerite Harmon. *When Children Ask.* New York: Harper and Brothers, 1956.

In story form this book answers the questions of children. One chapter is on "What About Babies?"

Driver, Helen I., ed. *Sex Guidance for Your Child: A Parent Handbook.* Madison, Wis.: Monona Publications, 1960.

A valuable help for parents. The result of the experiences of a panel of four writers. No illustrations.

Duvall, Evelyn Millis, and Reuben Hill. *When You Marry.* Boston: D. C. Heath and Company, 1953; rev. ed. 1962.

Two authorities teamed up and provided a 466-page book to serve as a textbook in a course on marriage and family for those contemplating marriage. It can also be used in personal self-study for young couples before and after marriage.

Eckert, Ralph G. *Sex Attitudes in the Home.* New York: Association Press, 1956. Also available as a Popular Library paperback.

A paperback published from the original hard-cover book issued by the YMCA. It is interestingly written with many stories from life, although there are no pictures. A real bargain for 35 cents.

Feucht, Oscar E., ed. *Sex and the Church.* Vol. V of the Marriage and Family Research Series. St. Louis: Concordia Publishing House, 1961.

A study of the development of sex attitudes among Christian people, with a fine Christian interpretation of sex.

Grams, Armin, *Changes in Family Life.* St. Louis: Concordia Publishing House, 1968.

One of Concordia's popular paperback "The Christian Encounter" series in which the author seeks to stimulate thought and discussion on the changes in the family due to the changing culture of our day.

Hymes, James L. *How to Tell Your Child About Sex.* New York: Public Affairs Pamphlets, 1949.

A 32-page booklet in easy-to-read language for parents. Very good.

Kirkendall, Lester A. *Helping Children Understand Sex.* Chicago: Science Research Associates, Inc., 1952.

This 50-page booklet has helped many parents in understanding how to guide their children in sex education. Very well written.

Kolb, Erwin J. *Parents Guide to Christian Conversation About Sex.* St. Louis: Concordia Publishing House, 1967. 144 pp. $1.95.

Lerrigo, Marion O., and Helen Southard. *Parents' Responsibility.* Chicago: American Medical Association, 1962.

One of the five-booklet series. Intended for parents of young children of preschool and early school age. Attempts to prepare parents and help them answer the first questions.

Lerrigo, Marion O., and Michael A. Cassidy. *Your Child from 9 to 12.* Chicago: Budlong Press Co., 1964.

A 28-page booklet distributed by doctors to parents at the time that its companion, *A Doctor Talks to 9 to 12 year olds,* is given to the child. It describes the physical changes the parents should expect in this age group and emphasizes the need to understand the child's changing feelings. Excellent suggestions for parents.

Lewin, S. A., and John Gilmore. *Sex Without Fear.* New York: Medical Research Press, 1950.

One of the best books available for a couple getting married and seeking understanding and satisfactory adjustment in sexual intercourse.

Narramore, Clyde M. *How to Tell Your Children About Sex.* Grand Rapids: Zondervan Publishing House, 1958.

A Christian psychologist offers help for concerned parents in an easy-to-read style. He emphasizes the importance of right attitudes but does not give detailed information on sex.

Peale, Norman Vincent, *Sin, Sex and Self-Control.* New York: Doubleday and Company, 1965.

The renowned minister-author-lecturer Peale attempts to step from the "new freedom" into growth toward maturity. A good thought stimulator.

Peterson, James A. *Toward a Successful Marriage.* New York: Charles Scribner's Sons, 1960.

This book by a recognized marriage counselor offers suggestions to those about to marry and those already married. For parents it is helpful in their own marriage and sexual adjustments and offers good chapters on the child and adolescent in your home.

Schmieding, Alfred. *Sex in Childhood and Youth.* St. Louis: Concordia Publishing House, 1953.

A professor of a Lutheran teachers college wrote this book as a guide for Christian parents, teachers, and counselors to help them lead children into right attitudes. Many of the materials come out of a clinical study of 500 children, many of whom had sex difficulties.

Swift, Edith Hale. *Step by Step in Sex Education.* 19th print. New York: The Macmillan Co., 1958.

Through conversations of Father and Mother and their children Bert and Ann at different age levels, the book suggests ways of explaining sex.

Wessler, Martin F. *Christian View of Sex Education.* St. Louis: Concordia Publishing House, 1967. 88 pp. $1.95.

What to Tell Your Children About Sex. Prepared by the Child Study Association of America. New York: Permabooks, 1959.

Written in easy-to-read language, this paperback covers the questions which are often asked from infancy through teens with an explanation and suggested words to use as an answer. It uses simple line drawings of the human body and birth. Another 35-cent bargain!

Appendix

Methods of Contraception

The methods of contraception are listed here in decreasing order of effectiveness and/or desirability. The products are approved by the U. S. Food and Drug Administration for use as contraceptives. The list is taken largely from the pamphlet "Modern Methods of Birth Control," produced by the Planned Parenthood Federation of America, Inc., now known as Planned Parenthood-World Population. For more information write to them (515 Madison Avenue, New York, N. Y. 10022), or see such books as Alan Guttmacher's, *The Complete Book on Birth Control* (New York: Ballantine Books, 1963.)

FOR THE HUSBAND

1. The condom or rubber or prophylactic

The condom is a rubber sheath designed to be placed over the erect penis. It is harmless and reliable. The many brand names available at any drug counter are quite reliable since the U. S. Food and Drug Administration classified condoms as drugs and controls the quality. To achieve the greatest protection against possible breaking or slipping of the sheath during withdrawal from the vagina, the woman may use a contraceptive jelly or cream at the same time the husband uses the condom.

2. Coitus interruptus, withdrawal, or "taking care"

This refers to the withdrawal of the penis from the woman's vagina prior to ejaculation. From a medical point of view this is neither reliable nor desirable. The anxiety of its uncertainty may affect the enjoyment and lead to emotional problems. It may fail to prevent conception because of poor control, carelessness, or because sperm may slip out before ejaculation.

3. Voluntary sterilization

An operation in which the duct that carries the sperm from the testes to the urethra is severed.

4. Rhythm method

Refraining from intercourse during the wife's ovulation period.

FOR THE WIFE

1. Oral contraceptives

This consists of pills, hormonal in nature, taken cyclically to prevent the monthly release of an ovum or egg. If the pills are taken exactly as prescribed, this method is considered 100 percent effective.

2. Mechanical devices

a. *Vaginal diaphragm* — a soft rubber cover held with a metal circle is placed diagonally across the vaginal canal. It is inserted for each sexual intercourse.

b. *Cervical cap* — a cup-shaped rubber, metal, or plastic cup placed directly over the cervix or neck of the womb. May be left in for the interval between the menstrual cycle.

Both of these devices prevent the sperm from entering the womb and thus impregnating the ovum. A doctor must examine the woman, prescribe the size she requires, and teach her to insert it. Contraceptive jellies or creams are used with the diaphragm and cap for additional protection.

3. Vaginal contraceptives

a. *Jellies, creams,* and *aerosol foam* — bought without prescription at any drug counter. Placed into vagina with applicator. Designed to immobilize or kill the sperm.

b. *Vaginal tablets* — available at most drug counters without prescription. The tablets contain chemical ingredients that foam in the presence of moisture. The tablet is inserted into the vagina, where at ejaculation it foams to cover the cervix.

c. *Sponge and foam* — a soft plastic sponge which is dipped in water, covered with the foam or powder, and inserted in the vagina.

d. *Vaginal suppositories* — usually consist of a sperm-killing chemical in a gelatin capsule which melts at body temperature. It is inserted in the vagina a few minutes before intercourse, but the gelatin may not melt quickly enough or be placed so that the neck of the womb remains uncovered.

4. Feminine hygiene products

Many products are advertised for "feminine hygiene" and "cleanliness" but have little contraceptive value.

5. The rhythm method

This method is based on the fact that a woman releases an egg cell from the ovary once a month about 2 weeks before her menstrual period. This egg cell can be fertilized up to 48 hours after its release. Then its life span is over. The life-span of the sperm is also about 48 hours. By a careful counting of the days of the wife's cycle a fairly "safe period" can be established.

6. Voluntary sterilization

An operation in which the Fallopian tubes are severed so that the ovum and sperm cannot join.

7. New methods

A device which is inserted into the uterus and left there until a couple wants a child is called an intra-uterine contraceptional device — IUCD. A number of types are now being used, such as stainless steel rings, plastic spirals and loops. It is thought that an object in the womb prevents conception by triggering excessive contractions of the uterinal muscles and Fallopian tubes, which displace the egg before it has time to be fertilized or prevent implantation. Other methods under study are "pill" improvements and a possible immunization method.

8. Not recommended by doctors

Douches.